When Poverty's Children Write

Advance praise for *When Poverty's Children Write*

Solley's important work reflects her deep understanding of poverty and her extensive knowledge of writing instruction. Her book is a gift for teachers.

—Maryann Manning

Author of *Theme Immersion*

Drawing from her study of impoverished children and the dedicated teachers who work with them daily, Bobbie Solley eloquently reminds us that children of poverty need the same opportunities that all children need. . . . This book provides a firm foundation for both novice and experienced teachers of writing.

—Nancy Bertrand

Author of *Good Teaching*

Solley relies on the voices of children and teachers to describe their journey through awareness, dignity, and competence as developing writers. While this text provides readers with the rationale and strategies for integrating writing across the curriculum, the personal quality of Solley's writing reads like a storybook.

—Kathy Burris

Middle Tennessee State University

Solley takes us into classrooms where a wealth of meaningful literacy activity affirms the abilities, experiences, and hopes of all children and celebrates their accomplishments as writers.

—Karyn Wellhousen

Author of *Creating Effective Learning Environments*

When Poverty's Children Write

Celebrating Strengths,
Transforming Lives

BOBBIE A. SOLLEY

HEINEMANN ❀ PORTSMOUTH, NH

HEINEMANN
A division of Reed Elsevier Inc.
361 Hanover Street
Portsmouth, NH 03801-3912
www.heinemann.com

Offices and agents throughout the world

Library of Congress Cataloging-in-Publication Data
Solley, Bobbie A.
    When poverty's children write : celebrating strengths, transforming lives /
Bobbie A. Solley.
        p. cm.
    Includes bibliographical references.
    ISBN 0-325-00751-9 (alk. paper)
    1. Poor children—Education (Elementary)—United States. 2. Language arts
(Elementary). 3. Poor children—United States—Social conditions. I. Title.
 LC4091.S618 2005
 372.62'3—dc22   2005012135

Acquiring editor: Lois Bridges
Editor: Gloria Pipkin
Production editor: Sonja S. Chapman
Cover design: Jenny Jensen Greenleaf
Cover photography: David Farris
Compositor: Argosy
Manufacturing: Louise Richardson

Printed in the United States of America on acid-free paper
09 08 07 06 05 VP 1 2 3 4 5

Contents

Foreword

Patrick Shannon

> I ain't broke, but I'm better than bent
> All I need is some dead presidents.

Anyone who listens to the blues knows that people living with poverty have remarkable facility with language. Some teachers (certainly the ones who taught me at Minerva Deland High School) would frown at the verb in the opening phrase of this lyric, but they would surely marvel at the play with the metaphor for being without money. Bent means that you've got bus fare and coffee money—perhaps even enough to pay one bill. But you are without means to cover your expenses. If you're bent, then you're not broke—financially or spiritually. If you're not broke, then all you need is some dead presidents (folding money) to set you right. If you're broke or broken, then you need much more than money to make it through. Bobbie Solley writes about the lives of people who are bent, but certainly not broken.

The weight that the poor shoulder is heavy and getting heavier in the twenty-first century. The official poverty line was drawn in the 1960s during the War on Poverty, and it is based solely on an equation, which assumes that food costs consume one third of household incomes. Although that assumption could have been true in the 1960s, it grossly underestimates the current costs of housing, health care, clothing, utilities, and transportation. Now food consumes less that a fifth of the average budget. In 2003, the poverty line was set at $9,393 for an individual and was doubled for a family of four (U.S. Census Bureau, census.gov/hhes/www/poverty). Over 36 million Americans fell below the line (a 12.9 poverty rate)—14 million of them were children. The poor are spread across the country (Northeast, 6 million; Midwest, 7 million; South, 15 million; and West, 8 million) and types of residences (city, 14 million; suburbs, 14 million; and rural, 8 million). Eighty percent were native-born and can be classified as representing different races (White, 16; Black, 9; Asian, 1.5; and Hispanic, 9). Half of the poor who are eligible and able worked full or part time during 2003. Official poverty surrounds us no matter where we live.

The official line is set so low, however, that it hides the real numbers of American families in need. Another 20 percent of Americans are within one paycheck of insolvency, have missed multiple payments on bills, and/or were insecure in food or medical care during 2003. The official and unofficial poor comprise one third of the American public, and according to government statistics both groups are growing as more manufacturing jobs are exchanged for service work, which often pays the minimum wage, does not offer full-time employment, and does not often include affordable benefits. According to the Center for Popular Economics at the University of Massachusetts, the jeopardy line that defines the official and unofficial poor will soon rise to 40 percent of the population, unless the federal government changes its policies during the next few years.

Yet, the government is in full retreat from the War on Poverty, cutting budgets and eligibility for income, housing, food, and medical care supports. The retreat started during the Reagan Administrations and has continued without interruption since the 1980s. Only the economic boom of the 1990s saved Clinton's record on these matters. Currently, the Bush Administration is attempting to shift responsibility for helping the poor to private, often church-related, agencies. Moreover, officials characterize the poor as lazy, immoral, or stupid for not being able to take advantage of opportunities in the global economy, assuming that they are personally and solely responsible for their economic plight and future. Promoting this position, President Bush proclaimed that his education policy, No Child Left Behind, was his job's policy also. That is, students who become proficient in reading, writing, and math will automatically escape poverty without further government intervention or assistance. Such nonsense disregards the current needs of the poor, overestimates the types of jobs being created in United States, and shirks government's responsibility for the welfare of all its citizens.

Bobbie Solley implies a different relationship between government agencies and the poor. She describes teachers in service to the poor, learning to harness their facility with language in order to learn about themselves, their relationships with others, and the social structures that surround them, and then, to act on their new knowledge. Because these teachers cannot influence their students' financial status, the teachers focus squarely on students' spirits. Although they waiver on occasion, the teachers reject the popular notions about who is poor and why they are poor. Rather, they work from the premise that their students are ready, willing, and able to add their voices to the discussion about their future and our own. The teachers believe that these voices are necessary in a democracy.

The poor populate most schools across the country. The teachers at Somerville Road Elementary School demonstrate hope that other teachers and schools might engage the poor in ways that will ensure that they will not break. Bobbie Solley's description of their work provides us with a voice of hope that the poor will not even need to bend.

Acknowledgments

Without the help of many people along the way, this book would not have been possible. Race Bergman, my mentor and my friend, told me long ago to set a vision for myself. He told me to set it high, to find what I love, and to find a way to spend my time doing it. As I listened to his wise counsel and began spending my time doing what I love—teaching—I came in contact with children and teachers who taught me what it meant to truly teach and to truly learn. I owe a debt of gratitude to Race for believing in me, for forcing me to look beyond my own boundaries, and for allowing me the space I needed to explore my dreams.

Throughout the writing of this book a door opened to new relationships. I am glad I can count both my editors, Gloria Pipkin and Lois Bridges, as new friends and colleagues. Thank you, Gloria, for your tireless reading and rereading of my manuscript, for your words of encouragement, for your support when I became discouraged, and for your praise when I had done something particularly well. Thank you, Lois, for believing in this book from the very beginning, believing in the need for books such as this to give voice to the many children living in poverty. Thank you for your wise counsel on difficult issues that came up during the process.

To newly acquired friends who had an impact on me and my thinking and writing, I want to say thank you: to Katherine, for reading my manuscript and giving me such crucial feedback concerning the knowledge we can gain from children of poverty if we will only take the time; to Randy, for giving me insight into how writing can be used for social action and how writer's notebooks can be used for much more than I had ever dreamed possible.

And to my true and faithful friends who listened to me as I wrote and offered valuable feedback and encouragement along the way: to Susan and Phillip, Tammie, Connie, Kathy, Karyn, and Nancy, I say thank you. Thank you for always being there for me.

My biggest thanks, however, go to the children and teachers at Somerville Road Elementary School. At a time in my life when I had become content to let the world go by and be a silent onlooker to the tragedies around me, the children and teachers at Somerville Road taught me what it means to be human. They forced me out of my comfort zone and in so doing, taught me the true meaning of life. I dedicate this book to them—the teachers who dedicate their lives to teaching and the children who will prosper because they have been given a chance to grow.

Introduction

Poverty. Children of poverty. Children from disenfranchised homes. Who are they? What do we really know about them? What beliefs do we hold concerning their lives? What biases do we have? And, perhaps most important, how do we respond to children whose lives are different from the middle-class norms we are accustomed to?

Our nation's schools have always served children from low socioeconomic homes. But since the implementation of No Child Left Behind and its reliance on standardized test scores focusing on subgroups of children, more attention has been placed on those who come from impoverished homes. Test scores for this subgroup are consistently lower than for children in higher socioeconomic groups. Therefore, our views of these children's abilities have been significantly altered. We are forced to focus on what children do not know rather than acknowledge what they do know. We are asked to "correct" their weaknesses rather than build on their strengths. In so doing, we rob these children of the potential learning that could occur. They come into our schools and enter our classrooms with experiences and knowledge uniquely their own. And yet, most of us hold misguided notions about their lives, their academic abilities, and their potential as learners.

I, too, was one of those teachers who had preconceived and misguided notions of what children of poverty could and could not do. I, too, believed that children from disenfranchised homes were somehow "different" and needed to be taught with these "differences" in mind. In short, I believed these children needed to be "caught up" with their more knowledgeable peers. How wrong I was and how misinformed I had been.

My change in attitude has been a relatively new one. It began in earnest when I happened to pick up Patrick Shannon's book *Reading Poverty* (1998). All my middle-class upbringing and beliefs were immediately challenged and tested. Had I been so blind all these years? The resounding answer was *yes*. Although my journey began during the reading of Shannon's book, it has not been an easy one. Giving up long-held beliefs about people, culture, race, and economic status has been painful at times, yet exhilarating at others. Perhaps the most significant event, however, to solidify my newly held beliefs came from actually working in a school considered one of poverty.

In the spring of 2002, Joyce Johnston and the staff at Somerville Road Elementary School invited me to become involved in the lives of their teachers and children, first as a writing consultant and later as an active member of the school. The children and their families have forever altered how I view learning in general and learning among children of poverty in particular. They taught me and continue to teach me what it means to live in poverty—what it means to feel hunger, what it means to fear losing your house, and what it means to lose hope. But more important, they taught me how crucial life experiences are to learning. Along with the teachers at Somerville Road, the children taught me how to look for their strengths in written language and how to use those strengths to build new knowledge. They taught me the art of true teaching and the joy of true learning. This book, therefore, is a testament to the teachers who work with children of poverty and to the children themselves who experienced the transforming power of learning in general and writing in particular.

Considered a school of poverty, Somerville Road had typically received test scores indicating that children were "behind" in both reading and writing. Reading, therefore, had been an emphasis for the past several years. Two newly hired reading specialists worked with students and teachers to implement a program known as Action Reading, which emphasized guided reading and reading for pleasure. Although Joyce and her teachers knew that progress was being made, that students were reading, they continued to struggle to show evidence on a test that children were indeed learning. The scores at Somerville Road were some of the lowest in the school district. By the spring of 2002, however, the efforts of everyone working together began to pay off as children not only read more and enjoyed the books they read, they also began to show evidence on the statewide standardized test.

Writing, on the other hand, had been left to chance. The teachers at Somerville Road, like many teachers around the country, *assigned* writing but did very little to *teach* writing. Children dreaded writing and teachers avoided it. As a result, the school had been placed on academic watch in writing. The teachers, support staff, and principal knew they needed help. I was hired in February of 2002 to become their full-time writing consultant.

The Children

Somerville Road, a neighborhood school, serves children who come from homes of poverty. Children in families living below the poverty line as well as in families considered "working poor" attend the school. The majority of parents hold jobs and work hard to make ends meet. In many homes, both parents work, but because the majority of jobs are low labor, they receive minimum wages, which do not always meet the needs of the family. Many children live in substandard and government-subsidized housing. During the three years I worked at Somerville Road, numerous families were unable to make their rent payment and were evicted from their homes, thus adding to the family's burden and anxiety in providing for their children. In addition, water and electricity were turned off frequently in homes where providing food and clothing took precedence over paying utility bills. During the second year I was at Somerville Road, several children's government houses burned to the ground, destroying all the families' possessions.

Somerville Road also enrolls a high percentage of culturally and linguistically diverse students. Thirty percent of the population is Hispanic, half of whom do not speak English as their first language. Twenty-five percent are African American, three percent are Asian, and forty-two percent are Caucasian. Ninety-eight percent qualify for free or reduced lunch.

Children's homes are characterized by various family configurations. Single mothers and grandmothers head many households. In other homes, other relatives such as aunts and uncles, grandmothers and grandfathers are the primary caregivers. A majority of children live in two-parent homes; in other homes several families live under one roof.

The Teachers

Twenty-three regular education, nine special education, two preschool, two Reading Recovery, and two ESL teachers, along with two reading specialists, make up the teacher workforce at Somerville Road. These teachers range in experience from first-year teachers to veteran teachers of almost thirty years. The turnover rate among teachers is low. I attributed this to the deep love, care, and concern teachers have for the children they serve. The job is difficult, however, as they work to overcome the challenges their children face. Teachers know and understand the lives their children live and constantly search for ways to access their knowledge and understanding in order to solidify the foundation they have. In addition to the regular staff, a host of aides and volunteers work daily with small groups of children as well as with individuals. Partners in education from the local hospital and church provide assistance in reading, writing, and math. As much as possible, children receive individual help at various times throughout the week.

My Work

I was hired to serve as a full-time writing consultant. My role was to help teachers at Somerville Road establish a writing environment to meet the needs of the children they teach. I introduced writers' workshop in a one-day in-service in February 2002. From February through May of that year, teachers formed self-initiated study groups and read Lucy Calkins' book, *The Art of Teaching Writing.* My full-time consulting work officially began in the fall of 2002. I spent two days a month from August through December in the school. I began conducting research in January of 2003. From January through April, I was able to be in the school eight to ten days a month. During the 2003–2004 school year, I continued my research and consulting work, which culminated in April 2004. While at the school, I interviewed randomly selected children from all grade levels as well as all teachers. I also interviewed six students and six teachers privately, in addition to conducting countless group interviews with both children and teachers. I kept anecdotal records of both students and teachers as they engaged in writing. I collected writer's notebooks from randomly selected children in every classroom and used these notebooks to chart progress. The teachers and I used this data to create, modify, and adjust lessons to meet the unique opportunities this group of children brought to us.

In the following pages, you will read the accumulated accounts of my work at Somerville Road. Throughout the book, authentic voices will be heard, and you will meet both teachers and children who will inspire and motivate as they come to rely on one another throughout the writing process. You will hear children's language celebrated as they engage in writing that has meaning and purpose. You will hear children's voices as they write from their own experiences and share those experiences with others. You will hear laughter and share tears as children write personal stories and poetry about the struggles they face every day. You will see children's language from home connected with their language at school. You will see some of the barriers of poverty begin to break down as children come to see the power that writing can have in their lives.

You will also hear teachers as they struggle to fight the demons of poverty and work to make their classrooms places where children feel safe and protected to write. You will see how teachers create positive learning environments where children learn to rely on themselves and on one another. You will see trusting communities established where children begin to take risks in their writing. You will see how teachers celebrate the approximations children make as they learn to bridge the gap between home and school. You will observe the techniques teachers have come to rely on as they work with children in writing—techniques that encourage children to think, to ponder, to interact, and to accept responsibility.

My knowledge and understanding of children from impoverished homes has changed because of my experiences at Somerville Road. My skewed notion of children and homes of poverty has changed. I have become more aware of my own biases regarding the poor, my own unfounded beliefs of parents and the desire they have for their children to succeed, my own misperceptions of the prior knowledge poor children bring with them to school, and my own inconsistencies with regard to teaching and learning. I continue to grow as I am constantly amazed at what children can show me when we put them first.

Poverty's Children

In late March, Missy Gann's kindergarten children gather on the car-
pet as they ready themselves for the morning. Everyone is talking at
once, vying for Missy's attention as she begins Morning News. "Eric,
tell me about your morning."

In his halting speech, Eric, a five-year-old African American child,
begins. "I'm jes hungry."

Eric comes from a home where his mother is unemployed and relies
heavily on government assistance. He lives in a low-rent housing proj-
ect with poor lighting, poor insulation, and very little furniture. He and
his mother sleep on a mattress in the middle of the living room floor
while his sisters share the one bedroom. Eric, along with his sisters,
receives his breakfast and lunch at school. On this particular morning,
they have missed breakfast. As Missy listens to Eric, he explains, "I did-
n't ge' up in time. My momma she didn't ge' up and I missed brefas."

Because Missy is using the speech Eric brings with him to school,
she writes exactly what he says, and then sends him to the cafeteria
for late breakfast. She moves on to another child.

On the other end of the building, in Amy Mount's fifth-grade
class, Ken sits with body slumped and eyes dazed as Amy begins the
morning talking about the reasons writers write. Ken has just lost his
brother. The death, due to an overdose of cough medicine, occurred
late one night in the family's rented house. With the help of neigh-
bors and friends, the family raised the money to bury their son. Ken
is a fifth grader who reads on a preprimer level and does very little
writing. Today is his first day back to school since his brother's death,
and for him, it is a place to escape the pains of home and receive
nurture, both physically and emotionally.

ric and Ken are but two examples of the millions of children who face overwhelming struggles due to the circumstances in which they live, circumstances not of their own making, but due to the hard times their families have endured. Many children come to school preoccupied with hunger, safety, and fear due to low-income and unsafe neighborhoods. In Missy's classroom alone, five children are Hispanic (three of whom do not speak English), seven are African American, and six are Caucasian. All eighteen children qualify for free lunch. In Amy's classroom of twenty children, six are Hispanic (three of whom speak only minimal English), seven are African American, and seven are Caucasian. All twenty children qualify for free lunch. All thirty-eight children have been classified as living at or below the poverty line and are labeled at risk for failure in school. By society's standards, all thirty-eight children are considered children of poverty.

Increasing Populations

Classrooms like Missy's and Amy's are all too prevalent in schools today. Demographics are shifting, and the number of children who come to school from disadvantaged homes is increasing.

RACIAL AND ETHNIC DIVERSITY

The racial and ethnic diversity in the United States has increased over the last twenty years. The Hispanic population, the fastest growing of any ethnicity, increased from 8 percent in 1980 to 16 percent in 2000 (Federal Interagency Forum on Child and Family Statistics 2002). Minority groups form the largest percentage of poor; Hispanics and African Americans are the largest two ethnic groups living in poverty. Hispanics, however, are 71 percent more likely than African Americans to be poor (Bonilla, Goss, and Lauderdale 1999). Children living in single-parent homes where the mother is the primary caregiver are 49.3 percent more likely to be poor than those living in two-parent families (Bonilla, Goss, and Lauderdale 1999).

CHANGES IN POVERTY RATE

While the ethnic and racial diversity has increased, changes in the overall poverty rate have also fluctuated. From 1993 to 2000, poverty in general decreased from 22 percent to 16 percent (Federal Interagency Forum on Child and Family Statistics 2002). On the increase, however, have been the numbers of children and youth living in homes of poverty. From 2000 to

2002, poverty among children increased. In 1964, 32 million people were impoverished; 13 million of those were children. By 1989, 40 million people were at or below the poverty line, and young people accounted for 39.5 percent of the poor (Reed and Saulter 1990). In 1995, over 5 million preschoolers were considered to be living in poverty while in 1999, nationally, one in five children, or 20 percent, lived below the poverty line (Bullough 2001; Sherman 1997).

EFFECTS OF POVERTY ON CHILDREN'S EDUCATION

Poverty affects children's later success in school (Bonilla, Goss, and Lauderdale 1999). Children "whose home activities, preferences, mannerisms, and understandings of the world do not align with the world are at a disadvantage in classrooms and schools" (Compton-Lilly 2004, 13). Therefore, children who live at or below the poverty line are more likely to have difficulty in school than are children who live above the poverty line. Poor children receive less health care, which contributes to excessive absences from school (Bonilla, Goss, and Lauderdale 1999). They are more likely to be hungry and suffer from fatigue, irritability, headaches, ear infections, and colds, which often lead to an inability to concentrate in school (Brown 1999). Because poor families do not represent mainstream ways of understanding the world, their children tend to experience high levels of sociodemographic risk factors in relation to later school success (Bonilla, Goss, and Lauderdale 1999; Moore, Vandivere, and Ehrle 2000). The level of parental education in low socioeconomic homes is correlated highly with educational difficulties among their children. The number of children in the household also affects educational success. As the number of children in the home increases to four or more, an adverse effect on education is evident. Finally, in families whose first language is not English, children have a higher instance of lower academic achievement.

Although poverty affects children's school achievement in general, literacy understanding, in particular, is affected more profoundly (Hodgkinson 1995). In some schools, children from disadvantaged homes bring with them a strong support system with parents who read and write, assist in learning, and communicate with teachers (Bullough 2001; Compton-Lilly 2004; Knapp and Shields 1990; Maniates, Doerr, and Golden 2001); in other areas, parents struggle to help their children (Federal Interagency Forum on Child and Family Statistics 2002; Brown 2001; Bullough 2001; Purcell-Gates and Dahl 1989; Sherman 1997). No matter the amount of support, there remain varying cognitive abilities among all children from disadvantaged homes. Some may lack a systematic method of exploration; others are quite adept at observation and discovery. Verbal abilities vary as do spatial and temporal orientation. Teachers recognize and agree, however, that all children come to school with certain ways of speaking with peers and adults (Bullough 2001; Compton-Lilly 2004; Knapp and Shields 1990). They all have methods of interacting, responding, and communicating. It is within this prior knowledge that literacy in general and writing in particular can grow and develop.

Literacy

Literacy can be viewed as the cornerstone for all current and future learning. It is through literacy that unknown places, people, and things are opened to children. It is through literacy that children explore their thoughts and understandings. It is through literacy that uncharted waters can be navigated. It is through literacy that children come to understand not only their world but also the world around them.

Although there are significant differences in literacy development between children from mid- to high-income homes and those from lower-income homes (Peterson 1997), all children bring to school with them some form of literacy in terms of reading, writing, and speaking. Writing is an area of literacy in which all children, regardless of socioeconomic status, struggle to learn. Yet all children bring strengths as well. All children know and understand how to interact within their home communities. Language abounds among children and their parents as they live and interact daily. It is from this knowledge of speaking and interacting that the foundation for effective writing can be built.

ORAL LANGUAGE KNOWLEDGE

Conventional wisdom would have us believe that children from poverty have no ability to converse with others, no language from which to draw, and little vocabulary; the vast majority of children coming from disadvantaged homes, however, do have a rich repertoire of communication skills and language. It is the differences between the casualness of language spoken at home and the more formal language used at school that present the greatest challenges to children from disadvantaged homes. Although formal schooling acknowledges and rewards specific word choice and conversation that involves both speaking and listening, children from disadvantaged homes are more skilled in nonverbal communication such as hand movement, facial expressions, and body language. Effective teachers recognize and build on the oral communication strengths of all children.

Donna Rauls understands the strengths children bring to her first-grade classroom. Eighteen of her twenty children qualify for free or reduced lunch, yet she recognizes the richness with which her children use their casual discourse while interacting with one another. Early in the school year, Donna takes advantage of this skill as she sits with her children and tells stories. Through storytelling, Donna capitalizes on her children's oral language skills. She models with her own stories by speaking briefly, including the major story elements, and using nonverbal cues. Children ask questions and begin to want to tell their own stories. Donna divides the children into pairs and story begins across the room. Her goal is threefold. First, she wants her children to feel valued. Through storytelling, children share and celebrate the experiences and stories of their lives. Second, Donna recognizes the skills with which her children come to first grade. She wants the room to be filled with children's authentic voices telling stories in ways that are comfortable to them, thereby helping the children feel success. Finally, because she begins where children are, she hopes to build on their knowledge of casual home discourse and eventually move them to the more formal register of school. Honoring the language children bring with them to the classroom then lays a strong foundation on which future writing experiences can be built.

PRINT KNOWLEDGE

Knowledge of print varies among children, depending on the social, cultural, and economic status of the home. All children have some knowledge of the written word based on their home environment. However, their understanding of how to use print to convey meaning may be different. Because many children living in poverty lack exposure to the type of print used in schools, they do not have a clear understanding of the reading-writing connection and the power that connection can have in their lives (Peterson 1997). Although print may be found in the home, the use of writing is scarce. For children like Eric, Ken, and countless other children across the country who enter our schools every day, print of the kind necessary to be successful in school may have little meaning to them. Although they may recognize the print in terms of McDonald's, Burger King, and Taco Bell, they do not come to school understanding that print conveys meaning. Many, however, see the need for print and writing in terms of being successful and avoiding trouble in school. Jacob, a third grader, sees writing as important because, "If I want to get a job, I'll need to fill out an application." Donavan, a first grader, believes that "If I don't learn to write, my mother will go to jail." Taylor, a second grader, explains that "Writing will help me pass to the next grade and I'll be smart." And, Marius, a third grader, says, "I get in trouble when I don't write so I have to write so I don't get in trouble." All four children see the need for writing but do not fully understand the power it can have to convey meaning and bring about changes in their lives.

Reading aloud to young children promotes language acquisition in both reading and writing. In lower socioeconomic homes, parents acknowledge the importance of reading to their children's future success in school and in life (Compton-Lilly 2004). For many parents, however, reading was a struggle in their own school experience. The methods they use to help their children are limited to techniques they remember: listening to their children read, telling them to sound out letters, and writing words they do not know multiple times (Compton-Lilly 2004). These parents are less likely, however, to read aloud every day to their children than are parents from more mainstream families (Federal Interagency Forum on Child and Family Statistics 2002). Books are evident in many homes of poverty, with the primary reading materials being newspapers and magazines. Children see their parents read and are encouraged to read themselves, but there is very little direct interaction and discussion about what is being read between the adults in the home and their children. When this occurs, meaning is affected.

As in oral language, children do come to school with prior knowledge regarding print. In kindergarten classrooms, children's language and knowledge of print is celebrated through the creation of centers. Jan Lowery, a veteran teacher of five-year- olds, begins her centers early during the school year. In her inclusive classroom, there are four children who do not speak English and one child who is nonverbal. The majority are in the scribble and prephonemic stage of writing. Nevertheless, she introduces the home living center by modeling how to play as well as how to use the literacy props she has included. She acknowledges that her children understand print at some level and promotes the knowledge they have. They recognize McDonald's, milk, and their favorite cereal. All these items are in the center. Empty boxes and cans from a nearby Mexican grocery store as well as from an American grocery store fill the kitchen area. In addition, Jan includes notepads, grocery list pads, cookbooks, recipe cards, a telephone, phone books, and message pads. She models how to use these items and expects children to use them as they play (see Figure 1-1).

In Jennifer Kirkland's fifth-grade classroom, she also recognizes the value in building on the understanding her children bring from home. Sanchez and José work together to write a story about their girlfriends.

FIGURE 1-1. *Kevin and Sandra at the kitchen center*

The boys describe the girlfriend in great detail while the plot of the story is virtually nonexistent. Dialogue exists in the story, but because nonverbal cues are hard to write, the conversation between the characters is simple. The boys' stories are indicative of most of the children in Jennifer's class. She applauds the boys' efforts at description, and for the next several days, she focuses on description in writing. She uses Sanchez and José's story as a springboard for helping children move from what they know and are comfortable with to what they need to know. Later she will do the same thing with dialogue.

Teachers who work with children from these low-income homes are faced with a daunting challenge. How do we build on the knowledge these children have? How do we help them come to love and appreciate the written word? How do we help these children come to see the power the written word can have in their lives?

Children need time for discovery and experimentation with print in order to understand its uses and power. Children from homes where reading and writing are used to convey meaning are better able to acquire the skills they need in order to be successful writers. Parents understand the need for children to play with words, play with sounds, play with books, and play with writing. Children who come to school from disadvantaged homes do not always have these opportunities. Therefore, school becomes the place where experimentation begins. Teachers must view instruction differently in schools that serve children of poverty. What do these children need? How can teachers provide the necessary background while helping them come to believe in themselves as writers? What can teachers do in order to assist these children in learning the power that writing can have in their lives?

Instructional Needs

In the past for children lacking knowledge about writing, instruction has focused primarily on the widely accepted technique of teaching the basics through skills-based, sequentially ordered curriculum that puts the teacher as the direct controller of learning. Proverbial wisdom and the current federal mandates (National Reading Panel 2000) would have teachers believe that if children come to school without the "basics"—letter recognition and sound-symbol correspondence—then they must go back and "teach" these skills in isolation. Teaching the skills becomes a rote memorization activity as teachers push children to remember the names of the letters of the alphabet and the sounds they make. The teaching of writing, then, can only be done *after* the skills and drills have been mastered.

Teaching writing in this manner does indeed keep children on task and gives them few opportunities for distraction. But when children come to school with a limited concept of print in the first place, rote memorization and skill-and-drill techniques do very little to help children see the purpose for print and the connection it has to meaning. It does little to develop the analytical or conceptual skills necessary to learn, nor does it do very much to nurture children's ability to express themselves in writing (Knapp and Shields 1990). There is less time for children to spend on thinking or writing. In this skill-and-drill mentality, students assume no responsibility for their own learning. They rarely interact with one another, thus prohibiting any learning that might come from others. There is, in essence, no connection to what is real and meaningful in a child's life; therefore, in this isolated mode of teaching, children of poverty never see any purpose or meaning in what they do. Skills-based teaching provides very little in the way of authentic learning, and the very essence of writing—writing to communicate—is lost.

When teachers come to understand and accept the strengths all children bring to school, they build on the purposeful, real communication that children bring from home. Focusing attention on the knowledge that children *do* have and the language they *can* use is the first step in developing a base from which to work. Rather than concentrating on the perceived deficits these children have, starting with their strengths gives teachers a place to begin where children's language is accepted and honored, and a place from which communication can grow.

Several principles underlie the writing instruction needed in schools of poverty (Cambourne 2002; Knapp and Shields 1990; Maniates, Doerr, and Golden 2001; Scheurich 1998).

ENGAGEMENT

Since the early 1980s, research has shown that the more time children spend engaged and "on task," the higher their academic achievement will be (Good and Brophy, 1994). Although no one questions the need for time spent on task, what constitutes time on task, however, has been debated among educators. Time on task for children from disadvantaged homes has meant "catching them up." As has been stated earlier, teachers perceive that a lack of skills in communication justifies instruction in isolated skills and drills. What is absent is the recognition of understandings that children bring with them and the purpose and meaning behind written communication.

Rather than spending time on skills-based isolated learning, teachers need to engage children in purposeful written communication. In successful classrooms, children see their lives as meaningful. They draw from the rich experiences that make up their lives and use their own language to communicate and interact with others. A communication-rich classroom environment also serves as the foundation for the process of writing. Children learn strategies writers use and put into immediate practice the techniques and strategies that experienced writers use to convey their message to an audience.

EXPECTATIONS

Schools serving children from disadvantaged homes establish high expectations and the belief that all students can succeed. Like children coming from homes where academic expectations are set early in their lives, many low socioeconomic parents want their children to succeed in school, get a good job, and even go to college (Compton-Lilly 2004). Others face daily survival issues of food, safety, and shelter and have very little room left for encouraging an academic future. School is a place where high expectations are set for all children. It is not enough to expect a child from an impoverished home to "just make it through the year." Teachers and children together set realistic expectations of using writing to communicate a message to an authentic audience and to make meaning and sense of their world. The expectations we set for these children grow out of the world in which they come.

APPROXIMATIONS

Children living outside the mainstream come to school with knowledge that may be different from children living inside the mainstream. Children may talk and communicate in ways generally accepted at home but these ways may not be accepted in school. Extensive vocabulary is often lacking. The difficulty they face in expressing feelings and emotions and understanding human motives and internal states of mind is evident as children speak and write. Yet it is vital that teachers recognize the strengths children have, celebrate the approximations they make, and applaud the growth as it occurs. Accepting approximations is a matter of building on what children intuitively know and understand.

Teachers create and maintain a supportive environment where all children are treated with love, appreciation, care, and respect. Providing a safe environment in which to write is critical if we want all children to come to know the power that writing can hold for their lives. Classrooms become places where children's voices are honored and accepted. Discussion creates opportunities for the real voices of children to be heard. Authentic audiences help children come to an understanding of the nature and purpose of writing for communicating a meaning to others. Providing a safe environment where risk-taking is respected and encouraged is the goal of every teacher.

CONNECTIONS BETWEEN HOME AND COMMUNITY

Finally, when schools exist for and provide service to the community, parental support for the school is strengthened. Connections between the home and school can be difficult in schools of poverty. In many instances, both parents work, and the ability to attend parent conferences and PTA meetings is missing. In other instances, lack of transportation, inability to speak to teachers in a common language, lack of confidence in their own abilities, and lack of positive past experiences with teachers prohibit parents from working in their child's classroom or attending school functions. Every effort, however, must be made to create a school environment where parents feel welcome and comfortable. Creating opportunities for parents to be in classrooms with their children while they write is a key component. Schools of poverty provide parents with a safe place to learn and grow themselves so they better understand how to help their children.

Only when teachers recognize the uniqueness of language with which all children come to school, whether they are affluent or underprivileged, can powerful writing occur. Discovering children's strengths and the richness of their language serves as a springboard for meaningful and purposeful writing. As children are applauded and celebrated for who they are and what they can do, writing becomes a powerful conduit for change.

"Writing is about speaking to the reader in ways that touch them."
Like Eric and Ken, Libby, a fifth grader, lived in a home where the strains of poverty were overwhelming. Relocated to a nearby foster care facility, Libby finds writing to be a way to escape the traumas of

her life, a way to come to terms with the abuse and neglect she had experienced in her home. The poems she writes and the insights she develops solidify the belief that children of poverty can indeed come to know and understand the power of the written word. "I write to share my thoughts. I write to let others know how I feel. I write to tell my story."

Building Trust
and Community

*On a Wednesday morning in Merry Wheatley's second-grade class-
room, Clarisse doesn't write. Wails can be heard down the hallway as
Clarisse tells Merry why she can't think of anything to write today.
Merry had asked Clarisse to pick up a tissue that had fallen to the
floor. Perceiving the request as punishment for something she felt she
didn't do, she sobs, "But, I didn't do nothing wrong. I didn't do it!"
As she takes great gasps of breath through her tears, Clarisse continues, "My momma always tells me how she never did nothing wrong
and she was always getting in trouble anyways. I ain't done nothing
wrong!" Merry takes Clarisse by the hand and, pulling her close tells
her that she doesn't think she did anything wrong. "Clarisse, you have
to trust me. I will not punish you unjustly. Please believe what I say."*

*On another day, first-grader Shiheka writes in her writer's note-
book. As she writes, three words per line begin to appear as columns
down the entire length of her paper. Confused and interested, the
writing consultant asks, "Shiheka, why did you write this way? It's so
interesting. Can you talk with me about it?" Shiheka immediately
tears up and starts to cry, thinking that she's done something wrong
and is in trouble. The consultant hurries to reassure her. "You haven't
done anything wrong, Shiheka. I was just interested in your writing."
She hugs Shiheka and continues, "I just thought it was an interesting
way to write. You've done nothing wrong. Please trust me."*

In schools that serve disadvantaged children living at or below the
poverty line, one of the main barriers that must be overcome in order
for effective writing to occur is children's lack of trust. Trust connotes
a feeling of dependability and predictability. Children learn to trust based
on their perceived notion of predictable behaviors from significant adults

in their lives. Through no fault of the children, low-socioeconomic homes are many times characterized by unpredictability, instability, stress, and anxiety. Financial hardships are created by low wages for those who work and a dependency on state assistance for those who do not work. Stress ensues as parents worry about where rent money will come from this month, whether groceries can be bought this week, or whether the water and electricity will be turned off once again.

Children, along with the adults in the household, carry the burden of survival. Although in mid- to upper-socioeconomic homes children grow up trusting that they will have a roof over their heads, food in their stomachs, and warm beds to sleep in at night, other children do not. They worry about their next meal, whether they will be in the same house from week to week or even day to day, and who will be at home with them in the afternoons and evenings. For many, their very survival is threatened each day. Family conflict results in a lack of trust within children. These children learn at a very early age that daily life is fraught with inconsistency, trust is often betrayed, and stability is elusive.

Yet, home is still the place where children long to be. And school is seen as a threat to their very way of living. The differences, the unspoken rules, the closeness, and the authority that all exist within schools can be uncomfortable at least and frightening at best. Mistrust is evident. Wariness and suspicion are the norms. Fear is often masked in unrealistic bravado. Aggressiveness is prevalent. Defensiveness is common.

Entering the world of school requires that children move out of their comfort zone and enter a world quite different from their homes. Rules of engagement and procedures for behaviors are different. Rules at home are always shifting to accommodate the changing dynamics that exist there. They are based on a daily fight for survival. School, on the other hand, with its rules of order, compliance, and routine, places children in a world they know very little about—a place completely out of their comfort zone. Although home may be a place of upheaval and turmoil, it continues to be the place where children have learned the rules in order to adapt. They have learned to survive. School and home, therefore, become two separate entities that children consistently battle to understand.

Children face difficulties each day as they try to balance these two worlds. Therefore, a loving, consistent community within the classroom must be maintained in order for children to learn to depend on and trust in the safety found within the walls of school.

The difficulty of balancing the two worlds of home and school is never more revealing and important than in the classroom where effective writing occurs. Writing, by its very nature, requires trust. It involves operations of the mind and spirit (Moffett 1968) that consist of putting one's thoughts together into words to be communicated to others, thus demanding a bond be formed among the children and between the teacher and the children. As children write, they open themselves up to scrutiny and inspection. Revealing themselves through writing, when trust is already low, becomes a challenge that teachers face.

Therefore, an atmosphere of trust and acceptance must be established within the classroom and school. Writing requires that classrooms be places where children are comfortable, respected, and accepted. They must come to believe they are valued for who they are and what they have to say. Teachers and support staff must work toward an environment that is accepting, trustworthy, and secure. A sense of community is vital. Trust, stability, consistency, and respect all begin with the tone that is established at the beginning of the year.

Building Community

To become writers, children believe they have something worthwhile to say and they learn to say it in meaningful and significant ways. Teachers build a sense of trust within the classroom as well as in the school as a whole. The school and individual classrooms become places where children feel safe, protected, and loved. The barriers that exist among these children in terms of trust, dependability, and stability are broken down in order for writing to occur. This is no easy task for any school, but for schools that serve children of poverty, the time and effort must be expended.

Building community begins at a schoolwide level and is supported by the principal. When writing is the focus, it is important that everyone in the building, from the principal to the teachers to the support staff to the children, come to know one another as individuals. Schools where community exists are schools where children feel safe to take risks, make mistakes, and learn from those mistakes. Schools where community exists are schools where adults are trusted to say what they mean and mean what they say. Schools where community exists are schools where children are respected and honored. Schools where community exists are schools where learning occurs.

Community begins with knowing one another as individuals. Knowing and understanding that children, teachers, principals, and support staff all have lives outside of school is an important component of a trusting community. Children are more willing to share their lives once they know something about the lives of others. How do teachers, support staff, and children come to know one another as people first? There are several ways to build community.

INDIVIDUALS MAKE THE WHOLE

It is important that children come to see themselves as individuals first and then second to see how their lives contribute to the whole. Teachers engage children in activities that focus on individual similarities and differences and how these work together to form a whole community.

1. **Puzzles of Our Lives.** At Somerville Road, Joyce Johnston believes in building community first among teachers and then among students. She begins the year distributing a puzzle piece made from butcher paper or tag board to her teachers and staff. Each person describes, through drawing and/or words, herself as an individual—free time enjoyment, hobbies, beliefs, and so on. As a group, the teachers and support personnel put the puzzle together. The puzzle is then displayed in a prominent place in the building for all to see. Once completed, teachers and children see that individual people with different and similar beliefs and habits come together to make the whole. Children in individual classrooms then create their own puzzle in an effort to get to know one another. They, like teachers, come to see how individual similarities and differences are important and contribute to the making of the whole.

2. **Museums/Showcases.** In some schools, teachers and children show themselves as individual people with unique interests and contributions to make to the whole. At Somerville Road, using a trophy display case, different teachers showcased themselves every month throughout the school year. Each teacher demonstrated the uniqueness of his life outside of school by showcasing various artifacts. Pictures of family, examples of hobbies, favorite music, favorite places, and favorite leisure activities were all displayed by teachers.

    Teachers brought their classes to see and discuss differences between and among teachers, differences and similarities that made each teacher unique and special. Comparisons were also made between teachers' lives and children's lives. This built a connection of community between adults and children that was invaluable to later writing.

Individual classrooms create a similar model. Teachers set aside a special place to house the museum. Each week two or three children bring artifacts to display in their museum. The selected children become the curators of the museum while others walk through, looking at the artifacts and listening to the stories behind each piece.

3. **Class Collage Bulletin Board.** In other schools, each classroom member, including the teacher, brings several personal artifacts that can be attached to a bulletin board. Each piece represents the person and might include CD covers of favorite music, book jackets of favorite books, labels from favorite soft drinks and/or food, pictures of family and friends, and evidence of beliefs. The teacher begins with her set of artifacts. Once she has described each item, she places them on a bulletin board. Each child then brings her artifacts and places them on the bulletin board. Ultimately, all artifacts blend together to form a whole. Discussions follow each day as the individual attributes merge with others in the class.

COMING TO KNOW ACTIVITIES

Children come to know themselves through reading, writing, and speaking. Teachers help children focus on recognizing individually unique characteristics of self through the activities they plan. Through these activities children gain a deeper understanding of themselves as well as of others. The following activities allow both teachers and children to experience episodes that lead to trust and respect within the classroom.

1. **Personal Cinquains.** Children in Mandy Brown's third-grade classroom follow a prescriptive outline to create a poem. Poems are shared and displayed throughout the room (see Figure 2-1).

   Line 1: First name

   Line 2: two adjectives that describe you

   Line 3: three verbs ending in –ing that describe you

   Line 4: a phrase that describes you

   Line 5: last name

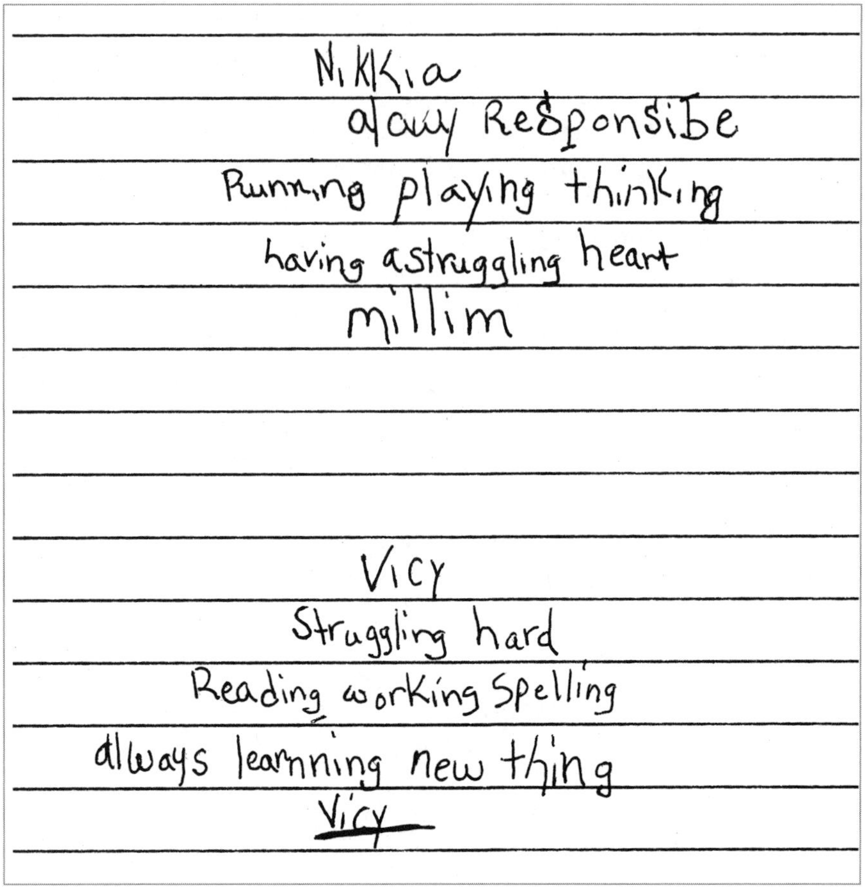

Nikkia
alway Responsibe
Running playing thinking
having astruggling heart
millim

Vicy
Struggling hard
Reading working Spelling
always learnning new thing
Vicy

FIGURE 2-1. *Nikkia's personal cinquain*

2. **Autobiographical Poems.** Children in Marissa Pedings' fifth grade follow a prescriptive outline to create an autobiography. Again, these poems are shared and displayed throughout the room (see Figure 2-2).

   First name

   Daughter/son of . . .

   Brother/sister of . . .

   Would need . . . (list three things)

   Lover of . . . (list three things)

   Who feels the need to . . . (list three things)

   Who believes in . . . (list three things)

   Who fears . . . (list three things)

   Who gives . . . (list three things)

Who would like to see . . . (list three things)

Resident of . . .

Last name

3. **Personal Acrostics.** Using letters of the first name, children in Mandy Brown's third grade write words that identify who they believe themselves to be. Once the acrostics are complete, each child shares. Through questioning and sharing, children explain why they chose the words they did.

4. **All About Me Books.** Children create flip books (see Appendix A). Children write interesting facts about themselves that might include favorite song(s), favorite book(s), things I like about me, favorite things about me, things I enjoy, things I'm afraid of, and so on. As the year progresses, other books are made that include deeper, more reflective aspects of children's lives. These might include issues children feel strongly about, inequities children see around them, passions children have, and areas of life they wish to change.

5. **Class Books.** Each child in the classroom contributes one page to a class book. Children may write and/or draw various things about themselves. Possibilities might include important facts, favorite hobbies, basic beliefs, family dynamics, and so on.

First Name	Vicky
4 adjectives	reader, talkitive, happy, runner
Daughter of	Jesus Garcia
Sister of	Ana Garcia, Alberto Garcia
Lover of	my dad
Who feels the need to	be quiet Sometimes
Would need	money to help people
Who fears	dolphins
Who gives	love to my family
Who would like to see	Selena
Resident of	Decatur AL
Last name	Garcia

Figure 2-2. *Vicky's autobiographical poem*

6. **Me in a Bag.** Beginning with herself as model, Brenda Taylor brings in a small paper bag filled with items that demonstrate who she is. Brenda pulls items from the bag and shares each one with the kindergarten children. She explains why each item is important to her. She might pull from her bag a seashell and tell about the time she went to the beach with her family. Or she might pull out a favorite toy she had as a child. Teachers who help children come to know themselves begin by sharing their own lives. Children then follow with their own bags, pulling out items and sharing them with the class. It is also good to have support staff such as the principal, librarian, and custodians come into the room with their own paper bags to share.

7. **Picture Cubes.** From heavy tag board, children make cubes (see Appendix B). On each side of the cube, children cut out pictures or draw items that represent who they are. The cubes are then hung from the ceiling in the classrooms.

8. **Scavenger Hunt.** Each student hunts for fellow students with unique characteristics. By asking questions of one another, students find out about each other.

All of these activities not only serve as ways for children to come to know themselves and others, they also serve to promote more active conversation and discussion at the very beginning of the school year, thus developing more meaningful oral language.

COOPERATIVE/COLLABORATIVE GAMES

Cooperation and collaboration are two components that make up an effective writing environment. For children of poverty, where survival is often viewed as fighting one's way to the top, cooperation and collaboration may be difficult. Therefore, teachers think in terms of fostering a sense of cooperation from the beginning of school. The classroom community is one where children feel free to ask for help and safe in knowing that their voices will be heard. There are numerous games and activities in which children can work together. The following are several examples:

1. **Wheelbarrow Races.** Jan Lowery pairs her kindergarten children together to form a wheelbarrow. Each pair races others to the finish line. This requires that two children cooperate with one another in order to win the race. If one child refuses to cooperate, the race is lost.

2. **Trap the Ball**. Two bedroom sheets (preferably twin size) and a ball are required for this game. Children are divided into two groups. Each group holds onto a sheet. The ball is put into play by tossing it into the middle of one sheet. The object is for children to work together to toss the ball from sheet to sheet. Children must cooperate with one another to keep the ball in play. Rules and means of keeping score are negotiated among the players.

3. **Ball of Yarn**. Children sit in a circle while the teacher holds a ball of yarn. The teacher begins by tossing the yarn to a child and telling one unique thing about the child. The game continues as each child takes the yarn, tosses it, and tells something unique about another child. The ball of yarn unravels as it is thrown thus making a web connecting all children together. This activity continues throughout the year and culminates in an end-of-the-year party where children talk about all they have learned about one another.

USE OF LITERATURE

The benefits of read-alouds have been documented for years. An increase in motivation to read, a better sense of comprehension, and an increase in vocabulary development are but a few. In addition, read-alouds are used to foster a sense of belonging and community. Reading books that directly relate to the children in your class contributes to the growth of a mutual understanding among children. Using books as a springboard for conversations encourages children to open up, share thoughts, and make text-to-self connections. It opens up the lines of communication between the teacher and the children as well as among the children themselves. It paves the way for respect and later the trust that must be present in order for effective writing to occur. In addition, the conversation that results from books fosters the oral language development necessary for school. Below are two examples of the type books that can be used and the kinds of activities that can follow. For a complete listing of books and activities, see Appendix C.

100 Dresses by Eleanor Estes is a wonderful book to read at the beginning of the year when discussions about respect and acceptance take place. Providing thought-provoking questions concerning the story and allowing children time to talk opens up discourse in the classroom. Once children feel safe to discuss books and the issues found within them, they feel safer to take risks themselves.

Feathers and Fools by Mem Fox focuses on the turmoil that can occur between different cultures when there is fear of the unknown. Small-group discussions explore the idea of ignorance and what it can lead to.

Community continues to be fostered throughout the school year. It is, however, what happens at the beginning of the year that sets the tone for future writing throughout the remainder of the year.

Setting Up the Classroom

Establishing a classroom where writing is prevalent and children's knowledge is valued requires time and patience. In order for children to become adept at "living the life of a writer" (Calkins 1994), the classroom is set up in ways that are conducive to living that life. Therefore, the tone of the classroom is positive, consistent, and predictable. From the arrangement of desks to the storage of materials to the charts on the wall, the tone of the writing environment is interactive and busy.

ENHANCING THE WRITING ENVIRONMENT

Several elements enhance the dependable, trusting environment necessary for children of poverty to recognize the knowledge they have and be able to write in thoughtful, consistent ways.

1. **Children's lives are valued.** Time is spent focusing on the lives and experiences of children as teachers ask questions and seek to find answers from those who enter their classrooms. Each year is new and different. Randy and Katherine Bomer (2001) remind us that each year brings a unique group of children with characteristics all their own. Getting to know a group allows a teacher the knowledge she needs to plan for the unique attributes of the children. The tone is then set for interest, acceptance, and understanding. Possible questions that teachers ask are:

Where do the children come from?

What is each child interested in?

What strengths does each child demonstrate?

What do the children do in their spare time?

How do the children spend their time outside of school?

What values do the children hold dear?

What celebrations make up the children's lives?

What is unique about each individual child?

What are the children's likes and dislikes?

2. **Interaction is valued.** The language children bring with them to the classroom is celebrated as teachers talk with children and as children talk among themselves. In many instances children of poverty lack the give-and-take required to carry on in-depth conversations where opinions are freely given and received. Because later writing requires listening to and giving suggestions, many teachers begin the year modeling and holding conversations. Ginger Wood, a third-grade teacher, sits with her children and tells them about her life—her family, her home, her children, the daily activities of her life. She encourages the children to ask questions and then models how to respond. In Donna Rauls' first-grade classroom, conversations about story are conducted and charts are developed as the children learn the rules of conversation.

    In both classrooms, as children become more familiar with the give-and-take of speaking, they take turns holding conversations for the whole class. Both teachers' goal is to help children become familiar with the roles two people have when conversing with one another. Later conferences about writing are enhanced because of the groundwork laid by Ginger and Donna in August and September.

3. **It is the *writer* who is valued rather than the *writing*.** In order to help build on what children come to school knowing and understanding about writing, teachers focus on the *writer*. Rather than focusing on the mistakes children make in writing, teachers celebrate what children are trying to say and do as writers. In Missy Gann's first-grade class, Eric is just beginning to put sound-symbol relationships together. When he wrote his first book, rather than focus on what he could not do, Missy celebrated with him the fact that he used writing in a meaningful, productive way. As a result, Eric continued seeking ways he could communicate his feelings through writing.

    For Missy and others, teaching the *writer* was not necessarily something that could be taught. It was something that had to be lived. When teachers begin focusing on the *writer* rather than the *writing*, they learn that it is not through *skills* that good writing emerges; it is in the daily *living with writing* that improvement is made.

    As she focused more and more on the writer, veteran teacher Donna Rauls stated, "I have totally changed my view of what writing is all about. It's not about teaching *writing* skills of capitalization and punctuation. It's not about correct spelling and sentence construction.

It's about what the *writer* has to say. All the skills will come later. The *writer* must come first."

4. The role of the teacher changes. In classrooms where writing flourishes, the teacher's role changes from dispenser of information about writing to one of observer, coach, and guide as she focuses on what experienced writers do and on what her young writers are trying to do. She is there to help and assist rather than direct. For many teachers, this is a difficult transition. Kindergarten teacher Missy Gann said, "I just don't feel like I'm teaching when I stand back and let my children figure out what they want to do and say. But, I've made myself do it, and I've found that they can do a whole lot more than I gave them credit for." She came to see that writing is not learned through direct intervention from the teacher, but through the watchful eyes of the coach as she guides her young writers.

5. **Print is valued.** Different types of print abound in effective writing classrooms. Tubs of books with clear labels depicting genre and style line the walls. Charts that hang on the walls and from the ceiling describe various aspects of writing from the job that authors do to the procedures for using a writer's notebook to the process for selecting a writing project.

FIGURE 2-3. *Eric at the authors' tea*

6. **Teachers and students ask genuine questions.** They then listen and respond in appropriate ways. A teacher who asks, "How do you play the game you mentioned in your writing?" truly wants to know and responds by actually playing the game. A teacher who asks, "What color is the girl's dress?" and responds with a "very good" is inauthentic in both his question and his response. As teachers show interest in what their young writers have to say, so their children begin to show the same interest in one another.

7. **Writing is a valuable endeavor.** Children acquire and maintain ownership and responsibility when they see that writing has meaning and purpose. Published pieces hang prominently both inside and outside the classroom. Fourth-grade students from Carol Mueller's class write pieces for their kindergarten partners and read to them in small groups. Donna Quarry's third graders write to authentic audiences as they share their pieces with community partners. Selected fifth-grade children read their original poetry over the intercom during the morning news. And the entire school celebrates with an authors' tea while reading published pieces to special guests (see Figures 2-3 and 2-4).

Teachers in schools serving disadvantaged children create classroom environments where the lives of children are honored, where risk-taking is supported and encouraged, and where authentic voices are heard.

FIGURE 2-4. *Salvadore at the authors' tea*

Connor, a student being raised by his grandmother, has never trusted anyone, least of all himself. Through the strong community built in Linda D'Antonio's fourth-grade classroom and the continued safe environment of Rachel Clay's fifth-grade classroom, Connor has begun to believe in himself. Issues of trust still exist in his dealings with others, but he has begun to trust in himself as a writer.

"Why do you love to write now, Connor?"

"I write because it makes me feel good to see that I can put what I feel and think on paper. I like for others to hear and see what I write. It makes me feel good." He continues, "I like to try new things. I like to write poems that don't rhyme and I like to read my writing to my friends. I think my writing is pretty good" (see Figure 2–5).

For Connor and the hundreds of others like him, a trusting, safe environment fosters writing that will both empower and help him transform the world in which he lives.

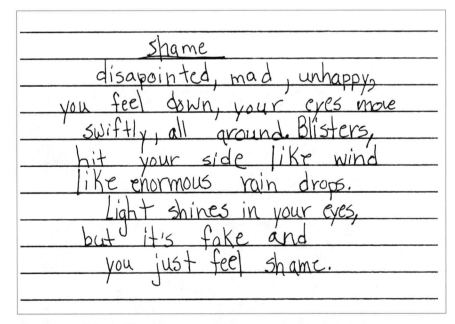

Shame
disapointed, mad, unhappy,
you feel down, your eyes move
swiftly, all around. Blisters,
hit your side like wind
like enormous rain drops.
Light shines in your eyes,
but it's fake and
you just feel shame.

FIGURE 2-5. *"Shame" by Connor*

Constructing Literacy
From the Bottom Up

In a third-grade classroom, Ginger Wood reads to her children each morning. As she reads, she watches her children for signs of misunderstanding or lack of understanding. One morning, she notices that Sam looks puzzled and asks, "Sam, what do you need help with?" He thinks a moment and replies, "I don't know that word you used— stool." Ginger asks for a show of hands from those who do not understand the word stool and many children respond. Amazed once again over the difficulty her children have with vocabulary, she goes in search of a stool so she can show her children.

"My momma, she having a baby and she get sick every morning and I wish she would be well cause she don't have no time for me when she sick." Reyesha is a third-grader who is quiet-spoken and shy. Mandy Brown, her teacher, understands the communication skills that Reyesha has as well as where she needs to go. Teaching, for Mandy, begins in the lives of children like Reyesha with the language they have.

Children come to school with a rich variety of language structures shaped by their family cultures. Traditionally, school has not been a place where children's unique language abilities are honored and respected; therefore, children themselves have been made to feel different and isolated within the classroom. Rather than celebrating the variations and nuances of children's language, many teachers disregard the strengths children have. Once again, teachers neglect to build on the language structures that are in place in order to hone in on the skills that may be lacking.

The word *build* implies construction: constructing a firm foundation to house language that will lead to power and transformation in the lives of children. Contractors begin with a clear picture of the whole—the ultimate shape the building will take. With their sights set on the whole, they lay a solid foundation and begin building from the ground up. In like manner, teachers become contractors as they solidify the foundation already in place and shape the structure from which all future literacy learning will take place. Teachers invite children to see the whole picture of literacy as they read good books, sing songs, recite poetry, encourage conversation, and allow time for play. Beginning with the foundation already in place, however soft and malleable that foundation may be, teachers build on what is there. They know that building on an artificial foundation where letters of the alphabet are taught in isolated drills and where sounds and symbols are practiced away from what is authentic will result in a faulty structure of language. They focus, however, on the basic foundation, searching for what is familiar to children and building toward what is unfamiliar. Teachers understand that in order for writing to flourish and have meaning, they must acknowledge and capitalize on the oral and written language children bring with them. As the foundation is solidified, construction of language begins to take shape.

Building Oral Language Structures

The use of oral language among children from disadvantaged homes puts them at greater risk for failure in school due to the casual register in which they speak and communicate. Language usage in schools requires that children use and understand a more formal language register where speech is clear, vocabulary is extensive, and norms of communication are understood among the users. For children whose language depends on general word choices and nonverbal cues and whose vocabulary relies on getting basic needs met, communication is difficult in school. Writing, in turn, is affected.

Finding ways to encourage talk and conversation presents challenges for teachers. In place of the interactive conversation prevalent among middle- to upper-class parents, poor and working-class parents tend to use more direct commands and demands (Delpit 1995). Once a command is given, children respond with some type of action. There is very little give-and-take in this type of conversation. When teachers know and understand the type of communication children are accustomed to, they are better able to capitalize on that knowledge and assist them in the building of more formal language structures. As oral language increases, written language also improves.

Different teachers use different strategies to help children build the oral language structures necessary for success in later writing.

MORNING MESSAGE

In kindergarten classrooms across the country, teachers begin the day with the morning message. Teachers use this time to promote community, language development, and knowledge about the world. Missy Gann is no different. The morning message is a ritual she uses to draw her children together and reconnect with them each morning. For many, Missy's classroom is a haven away from the chaotic lives they lead at home. So, the morning message serves as a reconnection back into the safety of her classroom. Missy understands the type of oral language with which her children come to kindergarten. She understands the body language and facial expressions as well as the one-word utterances that many children use. Therefore, her goals for the morning message are to acknowledge her children's language and encourage them to talk and express their feelings about the daily occurrences of their lives. She wants them to become familiar with the interaction that takes place between the speaker and the listener. As they talk, she listens and repeats what each child says. She then writes on chart paper for all to see the exact words used. As Missy repeats and records the children's language, she shows respect for what they have to say. Through extensive questioning Missy encourages children to think about and elaborate on their talk.

Sheri Costello, a special education inclusion teacher working in Jan Lowery's kindergarten classroom, also engages children in the morning message. Each morning a child is selected to be the star of the day. Sheri views this experience as a way to highlight every child in her room. She wants all children to feel special and know that their lives are worth sharing. Sheri also sees the morning message as a way to familiarize children with various forms of communication other than statements or commands. The selected child sits with Sheri as the other children ask questions. "What is your favorite color?" José asks. "Purple," responds Karen. Sheri acknowledges Karen's response and repeats it in a sentence, "My favorite color is purple." While Karen repeats the sentence, Sheri writes it on chart paper. Children continue to ask questions of Karen, trying to learn more about her. At the end of the morning message, the whole class reads together all the things about Karen. Karen takes the chart paper home that afternoon to read to her family. Not only does Sheri build communication skills among her kindergarteners, but she also shows them the relationship between speaking, reading, and writing.

The morning message is not solely a kindergarten technique. All grade levels use some form of the morning ritual in encouraging oral language and fostering a connection between speaking and writing. First graders talk about a baby sister or brother during share time while fifth graders talk about a memory they might use later in writing a memoir. Fourth graders make connections between a current chapter book being read and their own lives. Whatever the talk that goes on during the morning message, the teacher writes the oral speech either on chart paper or overhead transparencies. These talks are typed and sent home each day to be shared with parents. Each daily talk is copied and kept in the room, bound with others to create a classroom book of messages.

ORAL STORYTELLING

The story structure of children living in poverty varies. It is rich in its description of episodes, and characters form the center of the story. Expansive details are given and a series of events occur through dialogue. As has been stated earlier, Donna Rauls, a first-grade teacher, recognizes this foundation of story structure and begins the year telling stories. In language that children understand, she conveys meaning through nonverbal cues such as the use of hand movements, body language, and facial expressions. She knows what is familiar to her children and focuses on characters' conversations and the details of her story. She also understands that once a firm foundation is built, construction continues into the unfamiliar territory of expanded stories. Therefore, Donna gradually moves away from the familiar as she focuses less on the series of episodes that make up her story and more on the unfamiliar aspects of setting, feelings, characters, and resolution. Construction continues as Donna invites volunteers to share their stories with the whole class. Through questioning, wondering, and connecting, children expand their stories. With their increased knowledge of oral language, Donna places her children in pairs and storytelling continues (see Figure 3-1).

Paired storytelling serves several purposes. Children need time to converse in order for oral language to develop. The more time children are given to talk to and communicate with others for real purposes, the stronger their oral language becomes and, in turn, the stronger their

FIGURE 3-1. *Telling stories*

written language will be. Secondly, paired storytelling serves as a scaffold for later independent writing as children talk with each other concerning the stories of their lives. Just as construction workers utilize scaffolding as the building takes shape, so children need scaffolds in the construction of oral language. Donna uses herself and her children to support the scaffolds they are building through listening, asking questions, and making comments. In this way, she encourages children to think more deeply about the stories they tell. Paired storytelling also lets children know their stories are worth sharing. Stories worth telling are stories worth writing about. Donna knows that children write best what they know most about—their own lives and experiences. By honoring the oral stories her children tell, Donna says, "I want to hear what you have to say. I want to know about how you live and the experiences you have had."

BOOK TALKS

Planned, meaningful conversations in the form of book talks are the key to encouraging oral language (Kirkland 2004). No longer do teachers simply read books and ask comprehension questions about what was read.

Teachers know that grand conversations about much loved books not only enhance children's motivation to read but also encourage critical thinking and ways of speaking. The conversations fostered by books depicting critical issues of life allow children to explore their situations as well as examine possible solutions for circumstances seemingly out of their control. Teachers select books they know will prompt critical thinking and discussion. Books such as *Feathers and Fools* by Mem Fox, *Smoky Nights* and *Fly Away Home* by Eve Bunting, *Saturdays and Teacakes* by Lester Laminack, *The Other Side* by Jacqueline Woodson, and *Goin' Someplace Special* by Patricia McKissack all make for critical conversations among children (see Appendix C).

Unlike in many classrooms where teachers ask a question and the children give an answer, in book talk classrooms, teachers begin conversations. They may wonder—"I wonder why the foolish peacock thought the swans would try to make him swim and fly?" (*Feathers and Fools*); "I wonder why fences are used to separate people?" (*The Other Side*). Or they may question—"Have you ever wanted to go somewhere really special but were ⟩u couldn't?" (*Goin' Someplace Special*); "What could we do to help ⟩meless?" (*Fly Away Home*). By evoking critical thought and conver- ⟩on important issues that face many of the disenfranchised, teach- power children to think for themselves, speak for themselves, and themselves.

⟩na Quarry encourages her third-grade children to think more about the motives of others as she encourages conversation. After g *Singing Down the Rain* by Joy Cowley, Donna places her children e- to four-person teams. Each team responds to the question, "What ⟩ interactions of the adults sitting on the porch of the local store when the rain woman drives into town? Why do you think they behave the way they do?" By focusing children's attention on questions of why people in books behave the way they do, she fosters deeper discussion about the motives that underlie people's actions in their own lives. Through these discussions children not only increase their vocabulary and the ability to communicate and interact with others, but they also become more critical thinkers, listeners, and speakers.

STORY RECONSTRUCTION AND NARRATIVE COMPREHENSION

"The power in language development is in the revisiting" (Kirkland 2004). Although story retelling is a way for children to learn about language and the purpose behind it, it is in the retelling of favorite stories that oral language begins to grow. For many children, fairy tales, nursery rhymes, fables, and bedtime stories are unknown. They did not grow up on Mother Goose, Cinderella, and Aesop's fables. Yet, the language found in books of this nature offers children a unique view of story structure and vocabulary, a view that is missing in the lives of many children from disadvantaged homes. For many parents, reading nursery rhymes and fairy tales is a part of daily bedtime. But for children of poverty, bedtime reading is rare. Therefore, teachers introduce stories and rhymes in their classrooms that enable children to hear different language, play with words and sounds, and retell favorite tales. Teachers make an effort to locate stories, poems, and rhymes that all children can relate to—African American fairy tales, fables, and rhymes as well as Hispanic, Asian, and Native American stories are read (see Appendix D).

Retelling beloved stories through play builds vocabulary as well as gives meaning to purposeful conversations. After young children hear a favorite tale read many times, during center time, they use puppets to retell the story using much of the same language used by the teacher. In similar ways, dress-up centers engage children in the oral retelling of stories. By putting themselves in the role of others, children act and react in the safety of a trusting environment, thus preparing them for future situations they may encounter. Communication as well as problem solving is enhanced as children play together in their retellings.

PUPPETS

Betty Crandell uses puppets to help strengthen and enhance her kindergartener's use of oral language. Beginning in September, Betty uses puppets in one of her centers. Children are encouraged to play with the puppets as they talk with one another and as one puppet "talks" to others. As children become accustomed to the use of puppets, she adds speech bubble pages to the center. Children are then asked to write the speech of their puppets. In this way, Betty helps her children transfer their "talk" with the puppets to the written page (see Figure 3-2).

Older children use puppets to enhance oral language development as well. After reading fairy tales and fables, children prepare puppet plays for younger children. In the process, they write scripts, make puppets, create scenery, and rehearse parts. Not only are these authentic tasks for older children, they also enhance vocabulary and the use of oral language for different purposes for different audiences. Oral language is developed both on the part of the performers as they speak and the audience as they listen.

FIGURE 3-2. *Playing with puppets*

READERS' THEATER

Readers' theater is another opportunity for children to revisit much loved stories. It offers children the opportunity to convey meaning and feelings through oral reading and through the use of voice, facial expression, and hand gestures. Children internalize the written language of authors as they prepare for readers' theater. Oral dialogue in readers' theater promotes fluency and the use of language for varied purposes and audiences (Worthy and Broaddus 2002).

Children's literature offers ideal sources for readers' theater. Folktales, stories, and poems intended to be read aloud provide good material for oral interpretation. In addition, Aaron Shepard provides an excellent online resource for teachers interested in engaging children in readers' theater (www.aaronshep.com/index.html).

IMITATING TEXT

For young children, focusing on books with repetitive and rhyming schemes offers a unique opportunity for oral language development. The creation of imitation texts from predictable, rhyming books allows children to use the author's language in ways that are meaningful to them. In one kindergarten classroom, the teacher uses *A Monster Sandwich* by Joy Cowley to create a class book entitled *Monster Pizza*, with each child illustrating a page. In another classroom, *If You Give a Mouse a Cookie*, by Laura Numeroff, serves as a catalyst for a class book entitled *If You Give a Kindergartener a Crayon*, while down the hall, David Shannon's *No, David* is used to create a class book depicting children's own reasons for getting into trouble. The repetitive phrases and words help children develop a sense of language with its unique sounds and rhythms. Once the pages are written and illustrated, the book is prepared and placed in the reading center for all to read and enjoy (see Appendix E).

Older children also enjoy the repetitive nature of books. Like puppet plays they prepare for younger children, older children engage in imitative text creation as well. They create ABC books and repetitive books to be read to and by younger students. As children write for varied audiences and for meaningful purposes, both oral and written language are enhanced.

AUTHOR STUDIES

In Marisa Pedings' fifth-grade class, she encourages oral language for different purposes through author studies. After Marisa introduces Chris Van Allsburg, small groups of children select one of his books to study further. They work together to create a visual representation of the book to be presented to their peers. Some groups create game boards while others create book jackets, dioramas, and three-fold presentations.

Marisa hopes that by working in small groups to make decisions, come to consensus, and compromise, children use varied vocabulary. Different modes of language are used throughout the project as children work together and then present information to the class as a whole.

Activities and experiences that promote oral language development assist in the construction of overall literacy. The structure begins to take shape as layers of oral language are added to the existing foundation. Because children come to school with varying language structures, the shape of the building occurs in different ways and at different paces, but as it grows, so does language.

Building Literacy Print Structures

If we are to empower and transform the lives of disenfranchised children, we must encourage and assist them in associating print with meaning. It is in the interaction between the reader and the text that print takes on meaning and relevance. Due to the unpredictable and often chaotic situations in which many children live, time and opportunity for interaction about the meaning of print are rare. These children, therefore, begin school at a disadvantage.

Although making connections between meaning and print may vary, whether homes are rich with books or lack any printed material save the advertisements and fliers that come in the mail, children bring to school with them some notion of print. At Somerville Road Elementary School, kindergarten teachers note that approximately 25 percent of five-year-olds who enter school in August have never held a pencil, crayon, or marker; never colored or played with blocks; or rarely played in structured settings with other five-year-olds. While these five-year-olds may not use writing and writing implements, they do, however, come to kindergarten with a limited knowledge of print. Within the environments children live, they see food labels, printed advertisements, fast-food signs, and print on television, and in some homes they also see magazines, newspapers, and books.

Teacher contractors working to build literacy frameworks locate the foundations with which children come to school. As with oral language, shaping a child's print awareness and knowledge occurs only if the foundation on which it is built is authentically connected to what is relevant. Teachers face a monumental task each day as they work with children. Beginning with the whole picture of print through books read and poems shared, teachers find the foundation on which future writing can be built.

LITERACY DIGS

Betty Crandell, a kindergarten teacher, understands the significance of shaping the whole around a solid foundation of print awareness. Because her children have very little experience interacting with print, she begins her year with a "literacy dig" (adapted from the work of Denny Taylor, 1998). The purpose of the literacy dig is to help children recognize and acknowledge that print exists; it has meaning, relevancy, and purpose. The dig begins as the teacher and children actively search for print. The major objective is to help children come to understand the nature of print—its purpose, its uses, and its creator. Initially, Betty focuses on one section of her classroom containing various types of print. She gathers her children around a focal point and models the procedure she wants children to follow later. She (1) points to each piece of print individually, (2) names it, (3) labels it, and (4) discusses its use, its purpose, and its creator.

On the first day of the literacy dig, Betty begins with her children sitting around the door where several memos are posted (lunch menu, fire drill procedure, and tornado drill procedure). She points to the fire drill procedure written in bold, black letters and names it, "This says *fire drill.* It is a message we all must know. It gives us the steps we must follow if there is a fire in the school." She then reads the directions and points to each word as she speaks. Betty discusses its use (to help us know what to do in case of a fire), its purpose (to save us time should a fire begin in the school), and its creator (the fire marshal). She then moves on to the tornado drill directions and the menu, repeating the same process each time. Children ask questions and make comments throughout the dig. Betty continues the process in other parts of her room. As she does so, children begin to identify and define the print they notice. They talk about what the print might say, who might have written it, and why it might be important.

The literacy dig continues as Betty takes her children outside the four walls of the classroom and extends the experience in other areas of the school—music room, gym, principal's office, and so on. As she extends the literacy dig, Betty fosters a sense of print awareness as well as an understanding of the relationship between print and meaning to the children's lives. She then takes her children on walks outside the school building to explore print. Again, Betty extends children's perception of print and its authentic usefulness in their lives. Her ultimate goal is to invite children to dig for print in their homes. She invites them to find print and bring in examples where they once again name the print, label it, and talk about its purpose and creator.

Carolyn Dumas, a first-grade teacher, continues the idea of the literacy dig by creating a center. Within the center, she places sand buckets, shovels, and scoops. Hidden within the sand and sand dune area are various forms of print. Children use the shovels and scoops to dig for print and add it to their bucket. Discussion occurs among the children in the center as to the print's use, its purpose, and its creator. Samples of print might include newspaper advertisements, magazine ads, fliers, lists, and so on.

In addition to literacy digs, building print knowledge among kindergarten and first-grade children takes many forms. Teachers who work with children from disadvantaged homes use different strategies as they build on their existing foundation in order for effective writing to take place. Many of the techniques are familiar ones, but they have been misplaced and even lost because of the misguided notion that children from impoverished homes have no foundation on which to build. As has been stated elsewhere, when skills come first without recognizing the foundation that is present, the remainder of the structure is weakened and will forever remain faulty.

POETRY

Writing best-loved poems on chart paper and reciting them every day not only improves oral language but also builds children's print knowledge. Missy Gann uses a pointer as she guides children in the reading of these poems. After several days, children read the poem independently without the assistance of the teacher. They recognize familiar letters and words as they make repeated readings of poems (see Appendix F).

SONGS/CHANTS

As they do with poetry, teachers also write words to songs and chants on chart paper. As children sing, the teacher points to the words of the song. Jan Lowery and Sheri Costello use music throughout their day. Charts appear all over the room displaying the words to the songs/chants children love. This enables children to understand that what can be spoken can be written and what can be written can be read.

NURSERY RHYMES

Repeating favorite nursery rhymes helps children hear sounds and connect those sounds to letters and words. Teachers engage in repeated readings of nursery rhymes while pointing to letters and words. Children then read the rhymes during center time or free time throughout the day. Rather than focusing on nursery rhymes familiar to middle- and upper-class children, teachers use culturally appropriate verse to encourage both oral and written language. *Tortillitas Para Mama*, by Margot Griego, selected and translated nursery rhymes in Spanish and English, *Grandmother's Nursery Rhymes* by Nelly Jaramillo, *The Neighborhood Mother Goose* by Nina Crews, and *Chinese Mother Goose* by Ed Young are examples of the diverse nursery rhymes available to teachers (see Appendix G).

CENTERS

As has been mentioned earlier, centers equipped with literacy props enable children to practice using print in safe environments where approximations are applauded and meaning is recognized. Literacy props include anything that promotes meaningful writing and reading within the function of a particular center. The kitchen center includes telephone books to read and all kinds of notepads to write phone messages, grocery lists, and recipes (see Figure 3-3). The block center includes graph paper for drawing plans, construction paper for making road signs and building signs, and notepads for writing speeding tickets. A doctor's office includes a receptionist area with magazines and books for waiting patients to read. Doctors and nurses use writing to fill out prescriptions and make notes on patients' charts (see Figure 3-4). Puppet, card-making, label-making, post office, writing, and reading centers are added as the year progresses and as children become more accustomed to their use.

FIGURE 3-3. *Clarrisa writes a grocery list*

FIGURE 3-4. *Doctor's office*

Print awareness grows as children watch and play along with the teacher. Teachers who take time to play with children in the centers model the relevance of print. It should also be noted that centers are not solely used by kindergarten teachers. First- and second-grade children benefit from the use of centers. They are created with the children's background experience and knowledge in mind.

LANGUAGE EXPERIENCE APPROACH

A much-used technique to help children understand that what is said can be written and what is written can be read is the language experience approach. Teachers use children's own language as they come to understand the nature of sound-to-letter correspondence. With the help of her first graders, June Speake writes a piece about the trip they took to the farm, and Amy Mount's fourth graders write about the upcoming birth of her baby. In both lower- and upper-grade classrooms, children build print knowledge as they write for authentic purposes.

Knowledge of print as it connects to meaning is vital in strengthening the foundation on which children come to school. Through activities that assist children in connecting new information to their prior knowledge, teachers continue to build the literacy structures necessary to house all future learning.

Building World Knowledge Structures

Children write best what they know most about. Through experiences that comply to middle-class norms of behavior, children from middle- to upper-class families read the world in acceptable ways and write what they know best; they write what is familiar to most teachers and is therefore rewarded. Children who live in poverty also have a wide variety of experiences with the world in which they live. But these same middle-class norms suggest, however, that their experiences are somehow inappropriate and irrelevant to a classroom setting. In order for children to write what they know best, teachers acknowledge and celebrate their world experiences even when they are uncomfortable to hear.

Parents struggling to survive are often forced to limit their children's experience with the world outside their home. Meeting financial obligations, keeping food on the table, maintaining a job, caring for small children while trying to work—all have a profound impact on children and their abilities to see beyond the present chaos of their lives. Situations that middle- to upper-class children take for granted are experiences children of poverty are rarely exposed to—eating at McDonald's, going to a museum, seeing the ocean, noticing a robin dig for worms for her young, or watching a flower as it blooms. In homes where daily survival is the center of living, taking the time to observe and appreciate the world around them is a luxury parents can ill afford.

Yet, for children to write effectively with meaning and purpose, they must be able to read the world (Graves 1994). Therefore, teachers as literacy contractors help children observe and explore their immediate world in order to support the future writing they will do about their larger world. In order to help children with this task, teachers become familiar with the homes where children live. They know who lives with the children. They know the significant caregiver and her relationship to the child. They know what parents do for a living and how many adults work outside the home. They know the values families hold dear. And they know the traditions and celebrations that occur in each family. Working from this knowledge, teachers encourage children to talk about their own families and listen as others talk. There are numerous ways teachers engage children more fully and help them become better readers of their world.

CHILDREN'S BOOKS

Teachers select books that children can relate to, which depict various family configurations common to the situations children experience. Children see themselves in the books teachers read. They can relate to the characters and learn to view their world in different ways. Teachers recognize the diversity within their classrooms and read books such as *We Had a Picnic Last Sunday Past* by Jacqueline Woodson, *Miz Berlin Walks* by Jane Yolen, *Abuela* by Arthur Dorros, *A Day's Work* by Eve Bunting, and *A Jar of Dreams* by Yoshiko Uchida (see Appendix H). Teachers encourage children to compare families from books to their own families through the questions they ask: "How is this family similar to your family?" "What could you learn from this family that might help your family?" or "What could this family learn from yours?" In addition, questions that begin with "What would happen if . . ." or "I wonder why the author chose to . . ." allow children to think about motives and intentions in nonthreatening ways. Further extensions include the creation of charts and graphs that are displayed to demonstrate the comparisons drawn between various homes.

FAMILY TRADITIONS

Recognition of family traditions and celebrations offers children an opportunity to compare and contrast their lives to others. By looking at their own lives and comparing them to others, children expand their thinking and acknowledge a larger world outside their homes. After several days of discussion and reading about different families, Sally Connor, a third-grade teacher, asks children to bring in their family traditions and celebrations. Using this information, children work together to create bar graphs and Venn diagrams that depict similarities and differences. By engaging children in these activities, Sally helps them read their world and build their knowledge of the larger world around them.

ORIGIN OF NAMES

Parents name their children for various reasons—a family name passed down through generations, a favorite relative, a movie/TV/musical star, or a celebration of an ethnic tradition. Whatever the reason, names have significance in children's lives. Therefore, teachers like Kate Matthews and Christy Cameron invite their third graders to explore the origin of their names. Communication between home and school is enhanced as children ask questions about their names. Communication among children is enhanced as they discuss the origins of their names. And communication involving the larger world is enhanced as children explore their names. Children develop charts and use maps and globes as they search for their origins. Through this activity, children begin to view the world beyond their homes. It offers children an avenue for seeing not only the present but also the past as well as the future.

OUTDOOR WALKS

Teachers slowly move children from their familiar world to a larger arena of life. The foundation of children's world knowledge is further solidified as teachers take them on outdoor walks with the specific purpose of observing and exploring the world in which they live. Observation and exploration are limited concepts for children from homes where survival is the norm. Rarely do parents and children have the time or energy to stop, look around, and talk about what they see. Therefore, teachers demonstrate how observation is done. They show children how to stop and observe the small things—a bird's song, the smell of the air after a rain shower, or the inside of a flower. They demonstrate how to notice the big things—a broken down car in the street, dirt rather than grass in the yard, a squeaky front door screen, the color of a house, shutters on the window. And they demonstrate how to question why things are the way they are—"Why is one apartment building crumbling while another is kept pristine?" "Why do some houses have grass knee-deep and others have immaculate landscaping?"

Discussion follows each outdoor walk. The teacher's goal is not only to help children explore their world but also to encourage them to think critically about the world that surrounds them. Through questioning, the teacher fosters a sense of awareness and wondering, which later leads to problem solving and possible solutions to the inequities and unfairness of life.

WRITER'S NOTEBOOKS

A writer's notebook is a place to capture the world. It is a place to collect the seeds one gathers until he is ready to plant them (Calkins 1994; Fletcher 1996). Children keep writer's notebooks as they travel the world. They use their notebooks as places to think, to wonder, to ponder, to question, and to dream (Bomer and Bomer 2001; Calkins 1994; Fletcher 1996; Solley 2000). Keeping a writer's notebook begins with the teacher. It is the teacher who sets the tone for what children write in their notebooks. As teachers wonder and question and dream, as teachers share their insights about occurrences in their world, so children will use their notebooks as places to think and contemplate.

Lila Ackley, a second-grade teacher, discovered the power of a writer's notebook when she took her children on a walk outside the school. Somerville Road Elementary School is located across the street from the local hospital. On the day Lila's class was outside, a helicopter landed at the helipad. Doctors and nurses scurried about with their patient on a gurney. In less than five minutes, the patient and helicopter were gone. But, for days to come, children wrote about the incident in their writer's notebooks. They asked questions: "What was the illness of the person?" "Where was the helicopter going?" "When did helicopters begin to be used by hospitals?" They wondered about the patient's family, the survival of the patient, and the doctors and nurses taking care of her. Children's world knowledge grew as they contemplated life outside themselves. Their critical thinking improved as they thought about life beyond the immediate. Lila's belief in the power of writing and what it could do for children was forever intact. She wrote, "I had never taken the time to help children see another world. I had always tried to teach them what I thought they needed to know to succeed in school. It had never dawned on me that before teaching can occur, children have to have some knowledge of the big picture first."

GRAND CONVERSATIONS

As children increase their ability to notice things in their world, teachers extend these observations into grand conversations. Grand conversations involve both the teacher and children in talking about *big* ideas. It is the avenue by which understanding the world is traveled. Teachers hold conversations, demonstrate how to ask questions, and model how to talk to one another about underlying issues that might surface as children observe and critique their world. Bomer and Bomer (2001) discuss several techniques in building critical conversations about books read. Two of these techniques work well for holding grand conversations. Children meet with conversation partners to talk about observations made. These are quick sessions that occur in order to jump-start a fuller group discussion. They allow children who otherwise might not speak up the opportunity to talk in a less threatening environment. A second technique Bomer and Bomer (2001) discuss is a "fishbowl conversation." A small group of four or five children sits together in front of the class and carries on a conversation involving a critical inquiry into an observation made. The rest of the class listens, takes notes, or records information in some way in order to ask questions of the fishbowl group once the conversation is complete. Involving children in this type of conversation allows the teacher to more fully demonstrate techniques she wants all children to participate in.

As children become adept at observing, exploring, and critically thinking about their world, writing is enhanced. With a firm foundation of the world, writing about what they know best becomes an easier task.

Securing a firm foundation in oral language, print awareness, and world knowledge is vital in the building of literacy structures among children of poverty. Teachers who serve these children recognize the knowledge they come to school with and work diligently to set the foundation from which all other knowledge will grow. Writing, in particular, requires a foundation rich in experiences, firm in oral language, and secure in world reading. Recognizing thoughts and feelings that come from the heart and focusing on personal experiences and knowledge creates the authenticity necessary for writing to flourish.

Tomake, a fifth-grade student, shares his thoughts about writing. "Writing is about expressing your thoughts. It means to write your thoughts about things that happen in the past. It's about seeing your life and stuff and then writing how you feel about it." Tiesha, a fourth grader, agrees. "I write my own stories and sometimes I write poems. I write about things I've seen and funny things I've heard." Cameron Martinez also relies on his personal knowledge of language when he writes about his mother leaving.

All three children have begun to think about their world and to view it as worthwhile. They have knowledge about language that allows them to write from personal experience and knowledge. They have the confidence they need to write from the heart.

4

Structures That Teach

Eric enters his first-grade classroom, bleary eyed and dazed. Because Missy Gann has looped into the first grade with her former kindergarteners, she knows her students well and realizes that something other than the usual early morning sleepiness is bothering Eric. "How are you doing today, Eric?" Missy asks. Without preamble or emotion, he answers, "My house burned down yesterday."

In a kindergarten class, Dustin Lee sobs uncontrollably. Jan Lowery, his teacher, holds him in her arms because she knows that he has been taken away from his mother and now lives with a grandmother. His brothers have been taken to other relatives and Dustin Lee is all alone. He wants to go home to the mother he loves.

Children like Eric and Dustin Lee enter America's classrooms every day. Yet, learning is the farthest thing from their minds due to the situations they've just come from. Teachers often face overwhelming obstacles when trying to provide instruction to children whose homes are chaotic and unpredictable. Like all teachers, Missy and Jan work hard to provide a safe place for children to come each day, an environment where authentic learning can occur, and a classroom where children's knowledge and understanding are acknowledged and celebrated. They understand that to sit children in neat rows of desks and offer them static explanations of letters and words, nouns and verbs, and complete and incomplete sentences wastes precious time and energy. They recognize the abilities children have to prosper and grow, yet understand that instruction must change to fit their needs. Therefore, they accept the fact that teaching children of poverty requires a revisiting of commonly held beliefs, a rethinking of teaching and learning, a recommitment to building on the strengths of children, and a restructuring of the classroom environment.

Establishing Predictable Structures

Teachers face challenges every day as they build and maintain classrooms that meet the unique needs of children and are conducive to the teaching of writing. Building on the foundation of oral language, print awareness, and world knowledge, they create classroom structures where authentic writing takes place. Classrooms where children know they are worthwhile individuals with something to say and write are classrooms where teachers are consistent and trustworthy. Although children's lives are fraught with change, inconsistencies, and risks, teachers create safe environments where children's voices are honored. They establish writing structures that give children the security they need to trust themselves and others. Teachers create classrooms that demonstrate consistent patterns and predictable routines. They know that in order for writing to flourish, children need an environment where experimentation takes place without fear of retribution, where exploration is common, and where risks are taken and mistakes are made. They need an environment where they can do the work of writers.

Like children, teachers take risks as they establish a writing environment that allows children to take control and ownership of themselves and their learning. Teachers take risks when they allow children to keep writer's notebooks that represent their lives. They take risks when they allow children to select writing projects that have meaning to them. And they take risks when they focus on the *writer* rather than the *writing*. Risks however, are necessary in the evolutionary growth of teachers of writing. Without risks, teachers never explore the possibilities that children have to offer. They never discover the transformative power that writing can have in the lives of children. And they never come to know the potential that each child has for future learning.

SETTING EXPECTATIONS

Although Ginger Wood, a third-grade teacher, knows the risks involved in establishing an effective writing environment in her classroom, she begins the first day of school setting expectations and establishing structures for writing that will remain intact throughout the year. She tells her students, "We're all going to write this year. We're all going to be in charge of ourselves and the writing we do. We're all going to examine the writing that experienced writers do and learn to use those same strategies and techniques in our own writing." She understands that teaching writing is more than a set of subskills to be mastered or a set of prescribed lessons to follow. She knows that writing involves habits of the mind and spirit that can only evolve when children are actively engaged in their own writing for genuine purposes and authentic audiences. Therefore, Ginger establishes a set time for writing and on day one plunges into a discussion about writers and the work they do. Through her own writer's notebook, she demonstrates the importance of *capturing the world* and invites her children to write along with her. By methodically and consistently creating an atmosphere that demonstrates the value she places on writing, Ginger sets the stage for the future writing she and her children will do.

On the other end of the hall, Linda D'Antonio, rather than beginning the year as she has in the past, demonstrates her new expectations for writing by engaging children, not in discussions about complete and incomplete sentences, but rather in talk about their literate lives. "What is writing? What does writing mean to you? Why is writing important? What do you remember about your own writing? When have you written? Do you remember a time when you enjoyed writing?" Linda talks about her own writing life as she invites children to think of theirs. Together, she and her children create time lines to depict the various experiences they have had with writing. She focuses children's attention on writing, not just the writing they remember from grade levels past but writing for different purposes and audiences—writing letters and notes, making lists and sets of directions, labeling pictures and writing captions, keeping score and taking notes. Linda wants children to begin thinking of themselves as writers in all aspects of their lives. She wants children to recognize the important things they have to say and acknowledge the literate lives they currently have. By focusing children's attention on the meaning and intent of writing as a process, Linda sets the tone for the type of writing that will permeate her classroom throughout the year.

Betty Crandell greets her kindergarteners at the door on the first day of school. An easel sits at the door and children are asked to sign in as they enter the room. Some write their names while others do not. But all put marks on the paper. As the children walk into the room, they find tables filled with different sizes, shapes, and colors of paper along with pencils, pens, crayons, and markers. Betty invites children to write/draw and then later share what they have done. She demonstrates her expectations and value for writing from the first day her children walk into the room.

First-grade teachers expect children to continue their naturally developing sense of reading and writing. They demonstrate their expectations for writing for different purposes and audiences by creating authentic play centers. Children play in centers similar to those in kindergarten and continue to build on their knowledge of writing. Teachers add more complex tasks within the centers as they see the need. The kitchen center now contains not only cookbooks, recipe cards, and message pads but also sticky notes, grocery list pads, address books, magazines, newspapers, and calculators. Children play in a grocery store center that contains a checkout line complete with cash register, money drawer, magazines and newspapers for sale, along with canned goods, household products, and boxes of food. Children's roles in the centers change as they gain more experience with literacy. They engage in more authentic conversations and use more print to create messages that communicate with others. The purpose of first-grade centers remains the same as in kindergarten: to allow children the time they need to fully recognize the impact that print in their environment has in their lives, to understand the varied uses of print, and to view print as a viable communication tool. First-grade teachers realize that by establishing the importance of writing through centers, expectations that foster a deeper understanding for writing will continue throughout the year.

ARRANGING THE CLASSROOM

Teachers arrange their classrooms in order to create a structure conducive to writing. From the way the desks are arranged to the places writer's notebooks are kept to the procedures for conferencing, teachers establish writing structures early in the school year. Ginger Wood knows the structure and arrangement of the classroom will either promote or inhibit writing so she connects her third graders' desks side by side. She creates two rows of five desks on either side of the room facing each other with a set of desks in the middle. In this way, she creates an environment that matches her belief that children must be able to talk and share while they write. Fourth-grade teacher Linda D'Antonio and fifth-grade teacher Marissa Pedings both arrange children's desks into groups of four, while in Merry Wheatley's second-grade classroom, large round tables seat up to eight children. They, like Ginger, believe children need space and opportunity to share and talk about the writing they do.

Along with the desk arrangement, teachers establish a structure for housing children's writer's notebooks. Children need access to their notebooks both during and outside the time of writers' workshop, so teachers create clear procedures for their use. In Ginger's and Merry's rooms, children's notebooks are kept in a central location. Ginger places small crates on the middle of each row of desks; Merry puts crates on each table. The easy access at the tables and desks allows children to retrieve their notebooks throughout the day as the need arises. First-grade teacher Sue Newcomb places her children's writer's notebooks in a basket near the cubbyholes. When children need their notebooks, they are free to get them. Upper-grade teachers Marissa Pedings and Rachel Clay place a higher degree of responsibility on their children. They, like younger-grade teachers, also believe children should have access to their writer's notebooks as they need them. Rather than keeping them in a centralized location, however, Marissa and Rachel allow students to keep their notebooks at their individual desks and take them wherever they go. Rules and guidelines are set for appropriate places and times the notebooks can be brought out.

ESTABLISHING A WRITERS' WORKSHOP

Effective writing teachers introduce the writers' workshop and establish a set time and duration for writing each day. Setting a consistent time each day is important in establishing predictable routines. Children know and can count on the time each day that writing will occur. The amount of time teachers spend in a writers' workshop varies. During the first weeks of school, children participate in writers' workshop for twenty to twenty-five minutes, allowing time to get accustomed to the routine and expectations. As they gain confidence and skill as writers, teachers gradually extend writers' workshop to a full hour in all grade levels.

The structure of writers' workshop varies from grade to grade and from teacher to teacher. The format, however, consists of three basic components. An instructional focus lesson begins the workshop. During this five- to ten-minute time, teachers focus on specific techniques and strategies writers use when they write. Techniques deal with the *methods* by which authors craft their writing and involve the specific *ways* experienced writers use the conventions of writing. Just as an experienced artist demonstrates specific methods to future artists, so does the teacher share with future writers the *tricks of the trade.* Strategies are helpful hints and general plans of action that experienced writers use as they rehearse, draft, revise, and edit. Both techniques and strategies are demonstrated through the actual books authors write. Teachers then invite children to try out the technique or strategy introduced (see Chapter Five).

Because children need extended periods of time to write, the second component of writers' workshop consists of writing time. Just as swimmers train each day for extended periods of time in order to improve their skill, so should writers spend extended periods of time on the craft of writing.

Finally, the workshop ends with a group share time. This allows children to reconnect with other writers in order to receive feedback, share pieces, or gain additional information. Teachers make decisions about what takes place during share time based on children's writing for the day.

SETTING UP SPECIAL AREAS

The term *workshop* indicates a place where concentrated effort is expended on doing the work required to produce finished pieces of a craft. Whether it be an artist's studio or a woodworker's shop, the work that goes on inside revolves around that specific craft. Within an artist's studio, one might find storage for paintbrushes, canvases, and easels. There might also be a separate place for works in progress and another for finished pieces of art. In like manner, a workshop developed for the purpose of writing involves different areas where various aspects of writing are done. It is an active, living, breathing place where young writers do the work of writing.

Teachers and children together establish the different areas where the work of writing can be done. Students' desks/tables form the largest area of the workshop. It is here that children spend the majority of their time crafting pieces to be published and shared with significant audiences for authentic purposes. Writers need space where their thoughts have room to grow and mature. Therefore, this is a quiet area where talk is minimal. Here children spend time in their writer's notebooks as well as in the writing projects they choose to do.

Like an artist's canvas, the writing folders children use as they begin to work exclusively on a project are kept in separate areas of the classroom. These folders can be as simple as colored pocket folders or as complex as plastic, five-pocket spiral-bound notebooks. It is within these writing project folders that children draft, revise, edit, and prepare their writing for publication. Once children are engaged in the work of writers both they and the teacher set up other areas in the workshop as the need arises.

A revising area is established as strategies for revision are introduced and discussed. In a first-grade classroom, revision strategies are as simple as adding on at the end or adding description; in a fifth-grade class, children are encouraged to modify their leads or paint pictures through the use of vivid verbs and nouns. Within the revision area, then, young writers find lists along with examples of how other writers have used different strategies. Mentor books to assist them in revision techniques are also found within this area.

Writers use editing areas as they prepare their pieces for final publication. Here they find editing checklists, dictionaries, a thesaurus, as well as colored pens and pencils. Young writers read their finished pieces with the audience in mind.

Finally, workshops contain an area where materials for publication can be found. As children do the work of writers, many of their pieces will make their way into publication. Children publish writing in a variety of ways, from stapling their writing between two sheets of construction paper to binding hardback books with rubber cement and wallpaper. In some workshops, everyone publishes pieces at the same time, and in others children are free to publish when they are ready. Materials such as construction paper, rubber cement, glue, ribbon, stapler, markers, tape, and other items are included.

Teachers have similar goals in mind when establishing predictable structures for writing. All believe that writing is a more complex extension of speaking and a compilation of the experiences children bring with them to school. They all believe that writing requires time and instruction that is authentic. And they all believe that writing occurs as children do the work of writers. Therefore, they set up classrooms that not only establish predictable routines for writing but also create structures conducive to doing the work of writers.

Establishing Focus Blocks of Study

As teachers create writers' workshops, they face the challenging task of sequencing instruction in ways that are meaningful and authentic. They know that selecting lessons in the order of the language arts textbook is inappropriate, yet do not always know how to plan for instruction without that guide. In *Writing Workshop: Working Through the Hard Parts* (2001), Katie Wood Ray suggests a possible structure for thinking about writing instruction. She creates units of study focusing on various aspects of writing from recognizing the work that writers do to understanding and using the writing process to experimenting with genre. The units give teachers structure and a sense of direction. They give teachers time frames that assist them in making long-range plans.

When working with children who use oral and written language differently from what is typically accepted at school, Ray's units of study take on a unique perspective. After reading and thinking about Ray's units, teachers at Somerville Road Elementary School created their own blocks of study. While keeping some of the blocks intact, the teachers modified others and added their own to meet the unique needs of their children. In addition, the teachers at Somerville Road added more specificity to each block as they worked with them and became accustomed to them. In the second year of working with the blocks, teachers identified a sequence across grade levels that gave a more definitive structure to teaching. In Figure 4-1, a revised version of the blocks of study can be seen.

Blocks of Study

Preschool–First Grade

Block 1   Building a Community of Writers

Block 2   Environmental Print

Block 3   Oral Language Development

Block 4   Coming to Know Our World

Block 5   Who We Are as Writers/The Work We Do as Writers

Block 6   Types of Writing

Grades Two–Five

Block 1   Building a Community of Writers

Block 2   Who Are Writers/What Is the Work of Writers

Block 3   Author Studies/Reading Like a Writer

Block 4   Ways Writers Collect Ideas for Writing

Block 5   Writer's Notebooks

Block 6   Writers' Workshop

Block 7   Writing Projects

Block 8   Genre Studies

FIGURE 4-1.

Chapter Two addressed the first block of study, that of building safe, trusting writing communities where children feel free to take risks and learn from their mistakes. In this chapter, I will examine two other blocks of study—the work that writers do and ways writers collect ideas.

Children coming from homes where the connection between print and meaning to one's life is rarely made explicit may understand little about writing to communicate. Like many children, they do not see themselves as writers with important things to say. They view writing as something other people do and oftentimes equate skills such as recognizing the alphabet, drawing, or spelling with the actual act of writing.

"No, I'm not a writer, but my momma, she a good writer. She teach me how to write my letters," Cassandra, a second grader, informed me.

Dustin Lee, a first grader, thought his brother was a good writer. "My brother can write good. He draws good pictures."

"To write you have to spell good," said first-grader Ray. "Sometimes I spell wrong and have to erase and then I don't write good."

Connor, a fourth grader, agreed, "When you write, spelling all the words is important. You get a bad grade if you spell it wrong."

For these children, writing has very little to do with the content or the messages one communicates to others. Writing is something others do while utilizing a special gift or skill. Children do not believe they are capable of writing because the secret power of writing escapes them. The belief is further exacerbated when teachers perceive writers and the work they do in inaccurate ways.

Betty Crandell, a veteran teacher, confessed during the first year of implementation, "Writing, to me, had always meant handwriting and penmanship. I thought I had to teach children to write using good penmanship and then the first-grade teachers could do the rest."

June Speake, a first-grade teacher, agreed, "Writing has always meant teaching the writing skills of complete sentences and punctuation before any real writing is done."

Fourth-grade teacher, Linda D'Antonio, questioned the whole idea of writing as a process when she said, "Writing is about the skills. How can children write if they don't know how to write a complete sentence?"

These teachers, like their children, viewed authors as having special knowledge, secret gifts–spelling, punctuation, grammar, and parts of speech–that allowed them to write. Yet, in order to view writing as an avenue of communication, teachers and children must come to view it differently. They must understand the nature of writing. Rather than a series of skills that must be attained before any *real* writing is done, they must see it as a "process of using language to discover meaning and then to communicate that meaning to others" (Murray 1978, p. 86). They must understand the work writers do. Both teachers and children must recognize authors for the real people they are rather than mysterious figures who possess secret gifts. When children see authors as living, breathing, mistake-making people who struggle with writing just like everyone else, the act of writing is demystified. The aura and mystique of writing are taken away and young writers are left with the hard work and energy it takes to produce powerful pieces of writing. During the second block of study, children come to know writers for who they are.

Author studies enable children to know different authors—their lives, their likes, their dislikes, and their style of writing. Children then make connections between the work writers do and the work *they* will eventually do. The goal is for children to come to know and recognize authors and their style of writing and eventually use these people as mentors in their own writing.

Teachers begin an author study by introducing an author familiar to the children. The writer's family, favorite pastimes, pets, hobbies, and life experiences make for good conversations among children. Third graders learn that Jan Brett loves animals and has a house full of cats, dogs, and guinea pigs. Second graders learn that Robert Munsch writes about children he has met in his visits to schools across the country. Fifth graders learn that Patricia Polacco is dyslexic and did not learn to read until she was in the fifth grade. First-grade children find they can relate to Joy Cowley when they learn that she grew up poor in New Zealand.

Once the author's life has been shared, teachers then immerse children in the works of that particular author. Upon learning about Patricia Polacco, children read and examine *Chicken Sunday; My Rotten Red -Headed Older Brother; Thunder Cake;* and *Thank You, Mr. Falker.* Through books children gain a sense of personal ownership and relationship that allows them to view the author as a personal friend. And once children make friends with an author, they are ready to examine the techniques she uses in writing. Together both teacher and children analyze the ways in which the author uses words, phrases, and sentences to paint pictures in the readers' minds. They look at the author's use of structure in placing words. And they talk about and ask questions concerning the choices the author made.

In Mandy Brown's third-grade classroom, she introduces a new author every other day during the first few weeks of school. Rather than looking with any depth at the authors' techniques, she focuses at this time only on who they are as people and where they get their ideas for writing. As the year progresses and children begin to develop their own writing styles, Mandy returns to these authors in order to examine more fully their individual writing techniques.

In Marissa Pedings' fifth-grade classroom, the children begin during the second week of school studying an author's work in depth. Marissa introduces an author, Chris Van Allsburg. She divides her children into groups and each group is given a different book written by Van Allsburg to read and study the style, characters, plot, description, and setting. The groups share their information as they notice similarities and differences in the various books. The creation of a comparison chart culminates the experience.

As children become familiar with writers through author studies, teachers spend time focusing on *A writer is someone who. . . .* Together, teachers and children create charts that focus on the work writers do. They think about the activities writers may engage in. In Merry Wheatley's second-grade class, children view a writer as someone who writes, thinks, talks, listens, observes, and questions. Dot Neher's fifth-grade class sees a writer as someone who does all those things plus dreams, makes mistakes, reads, tries new things, learns from her mistakes, and takes risks.

By focusing on writers as human beings, children come to understand themselves as writers more clearly. They come to view their work as important—work that takes time, energy, and commitment. When they hear that Mem Fox struggled for over a year writing her newest book, *Green Sheep*, young writers begin to recognize the need for time and care with their own writing.

Ways Authors Collect Ideas

In Chapter Two, I discussed ways teachers help children use oral language for authentic purposes, become more aware of print and its meaning, and tap into the world knowledge that surrounds them. Through these techniques, teachers help children inquire into and discover the rich backgrounds and experiences they have. Once children are comfortable with the fact that their knowledge and experiences are worthwhile and valuable, teachers introduce new procedures for capturing those experiences.

Teachers and children across grade levels have used journals for many years. They were introduced in the early 1980s as a way to encourage daily writing (Graves 1983). Because children learn to write by writing, they needed someplace in which to keep that writing. Thus, journals became a common sight in classrooms across the country. They were places where brainstormed lists of topics were stored, webs of story ideas were drawn, and outlines of possible topics were written. Children wrote from story starters and prompts given by the teacher that had very little connection to their lives. Over the years, however, as we learned more about writing processes and the purposes for which we write, the journal began to take on new meanings. The term *writer's notebook* was used by Calkins (1994) to distinguish its use apart from journals. A writer's notebook is a place where writers "collect broadly" (Bomer 2004). It is a place for writers to capture their thoughts and ideas, use authentic voices, and record the occurrences in their lives. Teachers encourage their young writers to view writer's notebooks as "seedbeds out of which one writes" (Calkins 1994, p. 24), "containers to keep together all the seeds you gather until you're ready to plant them" (Fletcher 1996, p. 1). Notebooks, therefore, become places writers keep their wonderings, observations, thoughts, and plans. They are places writers record and question the happenings in their lives.

For children of poverty, learning how to use a writer's notebook becomes a journey of discovery. It becomes a journey of excitement and celebration as their experiences are recognized. It becomes a journey of ownership and pride as their life is accepted and applauded. It is through the writer's notebook that children come to see their lives as valuable, having meaning and purpose. Time spent at the beginning of the school year focusing on capturing the bits and pieces of life will later enhance the writing abilities of children.

Teachers do not tell children what to write in their writer's notebooks. Rather, teachers provide examples and strategies for using them. They introduce the writer's notebook by modeling with their own. They demonstrate the power of a notebook as well as the different ways in which the notebook can be used. As Marissa Pedings reads aloud from her notebook to her fifth graders, she notes how most of her writing is centered on her three-year-old little boy. Judith Looney, a fourth-grade teacher, talks about her writer's notebook as a place to grieve for the loss of her husband. Donna Rauls, a first-grade teacher, reads from her notebook about the things she enjoys doing outside of school. Ginger Wood shares with her third graders the questions she has when she sees violence on television. Through this modeling children begin to see the purpose of the notebooks.

Because children from disadvantaged homes have rarely been allowed to make decisions for themselves in school, the writer's notebook may be overwhelming to them at first. Giving them too many choices by saying "write whatever you want" can be just as inhibiting as telling them specifically what to write. Therefore, strategies for using writer's notebooks must be taught and practiced. Only when children have a repertoire of strategies at their disposal can the notebook be used effectively.

Remember the Past

Ralph Fletcher (1996) uses this strategy as he writes in his notebook. What has happened in your past that you will never forget? How did these things make you feel? Why will you never forget them? Cedric, a first grader, remembers the day his family went to Georgia (see Figure 4-2); Brittany writes about the day she entered the Children's Home. As children remember their past, they come to realize the impact their lives have had on the present. Their lives take on value when they are able to remember, write, and share circumstances of their past.

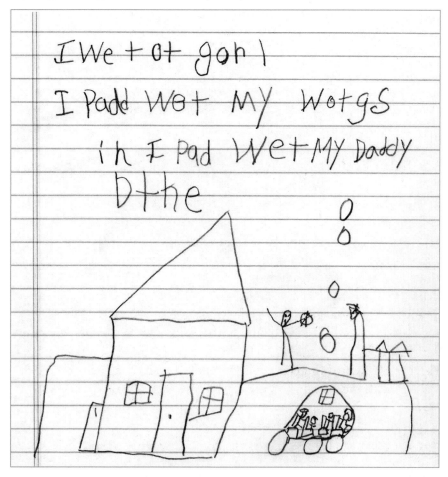

FIGURE 4-2. *Cedric writes about his trip to Georgia*

Teaching children to become aware of their world takes time and practice. As was discussed in Chapter Two, helping children notice their world increases both oral and written language development. A writer's notebook adds to that development as children capture the tidbits of life that have helped shape their feelings, emotions, and knowledge. Children spend time during the first six weeks of school practicing with their notebooks as they become more aware of their world.

Ginger Wood takes her children on a tour around the school. Because she and her children have studied author Patricia MacLachlan, they know that writers are users. MacLachlan says, "I steal everything. I don't get ideas sitting in a little room. I'll follow people an extra block down the street to hear the end of an interesting conversation if I think I might need it some day." Armed with her own writer's notebook, Ginger sets out to explore the world and notice anything she can use as a writer. She models how to stop, look, listen, and jot down interesting things she finds. Before long, the children begin to stop, look, listen, and write as well.

Lila Ackley's second graders also know that writers do not get their ideas by staying inside. She takes her children outside with their writer's notebooks, and they listen, smell, touch, and see all the things around them. They learn to make quick notes rather than long sentences and paragraphs. They will soon learn that what they have written in their notebooks will later become fodder for longer writing pieces. Because of their previous experience outside when the hospital's helicopter arrived at the helipad (see Chapter Three), Lila's children are more aware of the sounds and sights around them. Because they had captured the moments of that day, they are better able to focus on their surroundings.

Think About Your Emotions

What moves you? What brings you to tears? What makes you laugh? What makes you angry? What makes you stop and wonder? These are questions that experienced writers ask themselves as they spend time in their writer's notebooks. Clyde Edgerton, author of *Walking Across Egypt*, writes, "Being an author means paying attention to what strikes you. What you notice comes from your core. It's important . . . to be very sensitive to what is striking you." Teachers of young writers model how to capture the moments that move them. By writing in their own writer's notebooks, teachers demonstrate the emotions they feel when they see the first bud of spring, the first snowfall of winter, a newborn baby, a child in trouble, a car accident, or a house on fire. Teachers then create environments where children feel free to express those strong emotions.

Teachers encourage the sharing of emotions by reading moving pieces of writing—books that children can relate to and associate with. Books like *Chicken Sunday* by Patricia Polacco, *Singing Down the Rain* by Joy Cowley, or *My Mama Had a Dancing Heart*, by Libba Moore Gray evoke powerful emotions (see Appendix C). As the teacher reads, children talk about the emotions they feel. They then use their notebooks to write about the emotions and/or the memories the story invokes.

Emotions are also elicited through discussions and brainstorming sessions. Judith Looney, a fourth-grade teacher, gathered her children to the carpet in late September 2001. The discussion focused on the occurrences of 9/11. Rich conversations evolved as children talked about their fears, their anger, and their sadness. As children returned to their desks, they began writing in their notebooks. Powerful, emotional writing developed. Carrie, a fourth grader, shared her writer's notebook entry (see Figure 4-3).

In classrooms where teachers recognize incidents in the lives of children that prompt strong emotions, lives are validated. Children write and

My dad says I can't be

scared of the war.

But, I am.

My mom says why do we

go to war.

I say I don't know.

My sister says, it might be

coming to Alabama.

Her friend, Raven, cried.

I say the war won't come

to Alabama.

I say let's pray.

FIGURE 4-3. *Carrie writes about 9/11*

share their thoughts and feelings as their writer's notebooks become places to store these emotional tidbits.

Just as trust, risk-taking, and respect cannot occur until a strong community of learners has been established in the classroom, neither can effective writing occur until children understand the use of writer's notebooks. For most children, however, the idea of capturing life with all its tragedies, battles, victories, and lessons will be new to them. Therefore, time and energy must be expended at the beginning of the year. Yet time and energy alone will not create writers. Critical to the success of writer's notebooks is the teacher. Teachers must be writers themselves. They must write daily in their writer's notebook. They must share with children their own wonderings and questions. They must demonstrate their own struggles and confusion. And they must be willing to take risks in their writing just as they ask children to do. There is no better teacher of the writer than one who treasures her own writer's notebook and models the power that writing can have. Children in classrooms where teachers lay this type of groundwork during the first six weeks of school are children who write powerful pieces of writing throughout the year.

Conclusion

Children from homes where poverty exists often live in turmoil, upheaval, and chaos. They live in homes where daily life is unpredictable, where change is normal, and anxiety is constant. Teachers who serve these children, therefore, must create classroom structures and routines that are consistent and predictable. In order for writing to occur, children need an environment that is dependable, one they can count on to remain the same every day. As environments are created, both teachers and children take risks as they begin the work of writers. But, with time and practice, both become comfortable in the routines that have been established. From the structure of the classroom to the use of writer's notebooks, children and teachers come to respect themselves as writers with powerful messages to share—messages that represent the thoughts, feelings, and very lives of the young writers.

After Eric shares with Missy about the fire at his house, she gathers her first graders together on the carpet. Because of the strong community that had been built and the structures that had been established, Eric talks to his classmates about the fire. Silence permeates the room as Eric talks. The children then ask questions and express sympathy and support. As the day progresses, powerful, emotional pieces of writing emerge in the children's notebooks. Eric, a child who struggled with writing since entering kindergarten, has no trouble that day writing about his house and his feelings (see Figure 4–4). Brandon, one of Eric's classmates, is so moved by the incident that he writes a letter to Eric (see Figure 4–5).

Missy understands the structures and routines her children need in order to share and to write. By establishing these structures early in the year, she set the tone for the sharing and writing her children would do throughout the year. She gives children like Eric and Brandon voices—voices to understand their world, voices to reflect their thoughts, voices to transform their lives.

FIGURE 4-4A. *Eric writes about the fire*

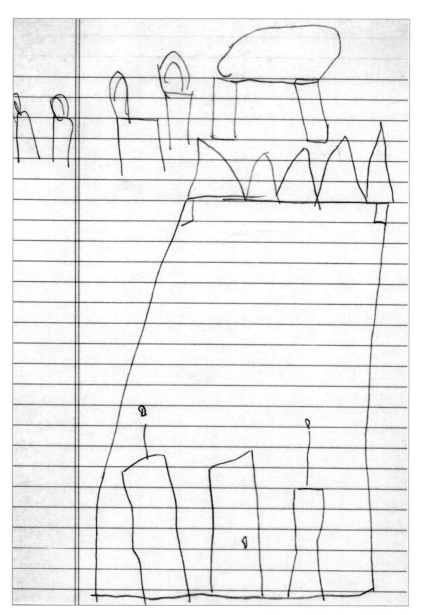

FIGURE 4-4B. *Continued*

FIGURE 4-5. *Brandon writes to Eric*

Instruction

On a morning in late April, Courtney's voice can be heard through-out the gym. A fifth grader in Marissa Pedings' class, she has been asked to read one of her poems to the school during morning assembly. With a shaky voice that grows stronger with each phrase, Courtney reads the poem that describes her life in a foster care group home. As she finishes the reading, a moment of silence is followed by thunderous applause. She smiles because she knows that the message she wanted to convey through her poetry has been heard. She later states, "Writing is about speaking to the audience. As a writer, I have to include details so my audience will understand. I write poems and personal stuff. I want my audience to know about me and maybe if they are like me, it will make them feel better."

Courtney knew that her writing had power. Marissa had instilled in her the belief that she was a writer with important things to say. She found that through writing, the fears and heartaches of living away from her family could be voiced and then shared with others. Marissa encouraged Courtney to write from the heart and then taught her the strategies, techniques, and conventions she needed to carry her message to an audience.

Writing to think. Writing to communicate. Writing to share. Due to the type of interaction with print that many mainstream children have experienced prior to entering school, they are more apt to embrace these purposes for writing. In homes of poverty, however, children have not had the same type of interaction with print and, therefore, lack the fundamental understanding that writing can relay meaning. Although many impoverished parents realize the impact that learning to read and write can have on future success, the methods they use to help children are limited to methods they know and understand. They may encourage their children to read and sound out words, but they engage in very little direct interaction concerning the meaning of what has been seen or read. Likewise, they may encourage children to write, but the methods used are ones they remember from school, methods that were inappropriate then and are inappropriate now: writing letters of the alphabet on lined paper or writing unknown words multiple times. As with reading, there is very little focus on writing to communicate.

Because teachers understand the limitations with which children come to school, they provide opportunities for children to write in ways that help them think, communicate, and share. They focus on the conventions *only* as children begin to understand the true meaning of writing. Children no longer spend their time writing a letter of the week ten times each on lined paper. They no longer spend their time underlining nouns and circling verbs in sentences from the textbook. They no longer recite various sounds that individual letters make nor do they memorize the definitions and rules of grammar and punctuation. What children *do* spend their time on is experimenting with sounds and letters, exploring the nature of writing, discovering the possibilities for topics, and practicing the art of writing for authentic purposes.

Teachers working in schools labeled at risk recognize the knowledge their children have, and therefore, begin where they are. Knowing that eventually they want children to use the process of writing to share messages with others, teachers begin with what children know best; they begin with their lives. Through oral storytelling, shared writing, and group stories teachers model the process of writing to convey meaning. They provide time for daily discussion and writing. They prepare class books of children's stories to be read and enjoyed by others. They model the process of writing through think-alouds. They demonstrate the impermanence of writing as they change sentences, cross out words, and add more detail to group stories. But, above all, they center children's attention on the meaning in their lives, they focus on the message to be communicated, and they teach children about the work that writers do.

In thinking about the work that writers do, teachers recognize that children of poverty do not always understand the nature of writing for meaning and the process that goes along with it. Parents who struggle with the daily trials of raising a family on meager income have very little time to interact with their children concerning the meaning that print might have in their lives and in communicating that meaning to others. For many children, writing is nothing more than words spelled correctly and put in sentences with periods and capital letters. Writing has no meaning outside the skills of grammar, spelling, and mechanics. The true power of writing is lost as they struggle to memorize the definitions of nouns and verbs, identify adjectives and adverbs, and practice spelling through daily write-offs.

In asking children what they believe writing to be, teachers uncover the inaccuracies many of them have toward the true nature of writing. First graders in Sue Newcomb and Donna Rauls' classes viewed writing not as the process of a meaning-making adventure but rather as a skill that had to be mastered. Many of them believed spelling to be synonymous with writing.

"No, I'm not a writer. I can't spell good."

"When I mess up, I have to ask somebody how to spell a word, and then I can't write."

"If I don't spell it right, my writing will be wrong."

When third graders were asked about what they believed writing to be, they too responded with similar misperceptions.

"You have to use periods and capital letters."

"You'll get a good grade if you use a period."

"If you write, you have to spell it right. If you can't spell, you can't write."

For children whose knowledge of writing rests with skills only, the very nature of writing as a process is lost. Teachers must work diligently to show them that writing is a process that occurs as meaning is conveyed to others. This process, however, does not occur in a linear, lockstep, sequential manner. Writers do not write in daily increments as they brainstorm possible ideas on Monday, draft on Tuesday, revise on Wednesday, edit on Thursday, and publish on Friday, only to repeat the process the next week. Teachers do believe that writing is a process of using language; it is a craft that develops over time, an art that is nurtured with time and patience as writers come to know themselves and the world around them. For children of poverty, this knowledge of writing is crucial in their growing abilities to write for meaning.

Teachers spend extended blocks of time helping children see their lives as worthwhile and valuable. They help children recognize that stories from their lives, however different they may be from mainstream lives, are worth telling. Linda D'Antonio believes that children's lives are the seed beds for growing stories and encourages Tierra to write about her grandfather's death (see Figure 5-1). Lila Ackley recognizes Cameron's need to write about the fight between his parents that resulted in his mother's

A Special Someone

I see
my
grandfather's angels
surrounding him.

I put my head down
and look
up.

It disappears.

Tears drip down
in a bowl
of water.

If only
my grandfather
could come
back.

Tierra, 4th grade

FIGURE 5-1. *Tierra's grandfather*

leaving (see Figure 5-2); Judith Looney encourages Bill to write about the wreck that killed a friend. Although all three teachers struggle with respecting children's need for privacy, they also know that writing can be beneficial as they work through the difficult situations in their lives. Because a strong, trusting community has been established in each classroom, children show support and respect for one another as their lives are shared.

Previously held beliefs that writing is a special gift that *others* have begin to dissipate as children of poverty learn to write with meaning. They begin to see writing as Patricia Giff, author of Kids of the Polk Street School series, does. "Writing is something you have to learn. It is a craft. It takes patience. I don't think writing is a gift. We learn to speak, we learn to read, not a special talent. . . . Writing is something you learn to do because you do it all the time." Children learn the true nature of writing as they are valued for the stories they tell, honored for the lives they lead, and rewarded for the risks they take. Teachers teach, model, and demonstrate that writing involves operations of the mind and spirit and is a process of making meaning to communicate with others. Judith Looney's fourth graders

---

My Family

Cameron Suarez
October 30, 2003
2nd Grade

My dad lays brick. He is a brick mason. I love him. He is a

good dad. On the week-ends he takes us to eat at cc's pizza. The

food is good there. Speshly the pizza. Me and my dad like pizza.

My mom ran away but we still see her. I spin time with her

sometimes. I love her. I hug her on my birthday. She even bot me a

football. Me and her play football together one time. We had fun. I

wish she could stay.

FIGURE 5-2. *Cameron's family*

see her heart and spirit revealed as she reads excerpts from her writer's notebook about the death of her husband. Ginger Wood shows her third graders that writing is not neat and tidy as she struggles to convey her love for her twins. She introduces experienced authors who tell children that writing is messy and in a constant state of flux. And once children begin to understand the true meaning of writing, teachers help them follow certain conventions in order to share that meaning with others.

All writers go through a process when they write, but not all go through that process in the same way. Experienced writers know that the writing process is not something they *do*. But, rather, it is something they *use* in order to create the writing projects they choose to work on (Ray 2002). Therefore, teachers demonstrate how different stages of the writing process can be used to convey the powerful messages children want to share. By focusing children's attention on the message, teachers show children how to live in a state of anticipation, aware of potential writing. Teachers further instill in their children that it is not in the *skills* that good writing emerges; it is in the daily living with a piece that effective writing evolves.

Before teachers can expect children to use the writing process to convey meaning to others, however, they first demonstrate how the process can be used. They do this through shared writing and group stories. Shared writing occurs as children experience and talk about their daily lives. Through morning discussions, first graders in Missy Gann's room learn about a fight that broke out between Dustin Lee's parents and the subsequent flight of his mother and brothers to the safety of a friend's house. Missy then uses Dustin Lee's story to engage the class in shared writing. Because she has encouraged her children to view their daily lives as valuable, no matter what that entails, she is not surprised that personal home life situations are shared openly in class. She has created a comfortable environment where children feel safe to share.

Missy has also created an atmosphere where children are comfortable asking questions, making comments, and sharing information. Dustin Lee feels good about telling his story again and with the help of the other children Missy writes. Once the story is written, Missy reads it, the students make suggestions and comments, and she demonstrates how to add additional information. On another day, she might return to Dustin Lee's story and the students will make further suggestions, thereby demonstrating the ever-changing nature of writing.

For many teachers, allowing and encouraging the sharing of personal stories openly in class is difficult. They worry that children may ridicule and mock one another or that parents might object to their personal lives being shared openly with others. But, for powerful writing to occur, children must come to value the stories they have to tell. As Donald Graves (1983) states, children write best what they know most about. Like children from middle-class homes, what children of poverty know most about is living their daily lives. Teachers encourage children from middle- to upper-class families to write about their vacation or their pet or their birthday party or any of a number of things that mainstream children engage in. Children of poverty also engage in daily activities unique to them, but many teachers fail to capitalize on the lives they live. It makes us uncomfortable when a fourth grader writes about running out of food stamps and having no breakfast. It makes us feel bad when a second grader writes about her family living in a two-bedroom apartment with another family. Like Missy, if we are to truly help our students see the value of writing, all teachers must recognize the lives their children live, value the stories they have to tell, and accept and applaud the messages they want to convey (Jones 2004).

Not only does shared writing help children value the stories they have to tell, it also helps children become accustomed to the fact that writing is a process that can be changed, added to, and modified. This externalization of an internal process helps children eventually use the writing process as they write individually. For experienced writers, the specific lines that separate the stages of the writing process are blurred. Because they live with writing every day, the parts of the process merge and coexist in their minds. However, children who are just beginning to live the "writerly life" (Calkins 1994) need to know and distinguish between the different stages of the process. They, like experienced writers, will eventually use the writing process to write their own powerful pieces.

REHEARSAL

Rehearsal begins as children explore their world. Their writers' notebooks become places where moments of life are captured, where bits of experience are remembered, where questions are asked, and where experimentation occurs. Rehearsal is a "state of readiness out of which one writes" (Calkins 1994, p. 23). Teachers constantly refer children to their writer's notebooks throughout the day. It may be from a book read aloud that teachers encourage children to jot down a feeling, remember a special time, or practice a particular technique. It may be in a walk to the lunchroom that teachers demonstrate how to stop and listen to conversations among other adults, to music coming from the gym, to the squeak of the mop bucket as the custodian pushes it down the hall and later write those observations in their writer's notebooks. Whatever it may be, teachers encourage children to "collect broadly" (Bomer 2004) and think about their lives as rehearsal for writing (see Chapter Four for ways to use writer's notebooks).

Both teachers and children keep writer's notebooks to store the seeds of life until they are ready to plant them into beds of poems, stories, or remembrances. Once they are ready to grow a story, teachers teach children to reread their writer's notebooks looking for possible topics and themes. The topic should be one that children already know a lot about or want to know more about. Teachers help children reread their notebooks looking for the one piece or the several pieces that warrant more time and energy. This part of the process is difficult for children, and teachers spend extended periods of time modeling how to select pieces from writer's notebooks (see Figure 5-3). Ginger Wood helps her third graders reread their notebooks by first modeling with her own; she reads and thinks aloud about the different entries she has made. She demonstrates how to ask herself questions and think through possibilities. She models the procedure multiple times with her own notebook and then asks for a volunteer to model with his. Stacie volunteers and reads entries while the class listens and asks questions. He asks for help as he tries to select the piece he wants to spend more time on. Through questioning and commenting, Stacie is able to think about what he knows about a topic and decide what matters to him most. Once a student has demonstrated to the whole class, Ginger puts the rest of her children into small groups. With no more than three children in a group, they read and reread their writer's notebooks to one another, following the procedure Ginger has established. The time devoted to rereading and selecting is vital to children's future writing abilities. Time spent in the beginning establishing routines of rereading and selecting helps children internalize the processes they will use throughout the year. The topic or theme selected becomes a writing project that children spend time developing.

PREWRITING

Once a topic has been selected, prewriting begins. Prewriting involves writing more as writers collect additional information about the topic. There are several ways that teachers help children write more.

Steps in a Writing Project

Step 1 I reread my writer's notebook with a specific purpose in mind. I look for an entry I want to spend more time on developing into a writing project or I look for several entries that pertain to a common theme.

Step 2 Select a topic or theme. It should answer two questions: "Do I know a lot about this topic?" and "Do I want to spend a great deal of time on this topic?"

Step 3 Once I decide on a topic or theme, I write more about it. I may brainstorm, web, outline, make lists, research more facts, or talk to other people.

Step 4 Once I have all my information, I build a vision for my text (Bomer 2004). I decide what type of writing I want to do. It could be a piece of fiction, nonfiction, poem, short story, narrative, letter, biography, etc.

Step 5 On a clean sheet of paper outside my writer's notebook, I draft my piece. I skip lines and only write on the front side of my paper.

Step 6 I spend time rereading my draft. I reread it looking for places that I might revise. I need to ask myself questions about my writing.

> What can I add to my piece?
> Do I need to take something out of my piece?
> Do I need to change some things?
> Can I make my writing clearer?

Step 7 I read my piece to a neighbor asking for feedback. I listen to the questions my neighbor asks me and decide whether or not I need to make any other changes.

Step 8 I edit my revised piece of writing using my editing checklist.

Step 9 I publish my finished piece.

FIGURE 5-3.

1. **Brainstorm.** Teachers show children how to clear their mind of everything except the topic at hand. Then they write as quickly as possible about everything they remember or know about the topic. The results may be in list form, sentence form, or paragraphs.

2. **Web.** Children learn to web their topic by placing the central theme inside a circle. Drawing lines away from the circle, writers include everything they can recall about the topic.

3. **Outline.** Teachers show older children how to outline their topic. This is particularly helpful when children write expository texts or research papers. Marissa Pedings, a fifth-grade teacher, uses outlining to help her students organize for expository text writing.

As with rereading and selecting, extended periods of time are spent teaching children different ways of prewriting. In this way, children build a repertoire of strategies from which they can draw on as they continue writing throughout the year.

Prewriting is important in that it helps young writers build a vision of the text they would like to write (Bomer 2004). Many teachers only talk in terms of story as they help children move from their notebooks to prewriting. But there are a multitude of possibilities when thinking of the particular text children might write. Teachers spend time introducing different text types at the beginning of the year. Throughout the remainder of the year, children add to the list as they come in contact with more texts. Kindergarten and first-grade teachers collect and label different types of books in tubs. Missy Gann introduces her kindergarteners to wordless picture books, picture books with captions, picture books with few words, and ABC books. She chooses these books because she knows this is the type of writing her five-year-olds will be doing. She establishes mentor texts for her children early in the year so they will have multiple options when thinking about writing. In like manner, Sue Newcomb creates tubs of books that will be familiar to her incoming first graders and then proceeds to introduce new types of books—books with many words on a page, fiction, poetry, nonfiction. Teachers at each grade level build on children's previous knowledge by creating classroom libraries where familiar labeled books are kept as well as new types of books (see Appendix I).

DRAFTING

Once writers have engaged in prewriting and feel they know a lot about their selected topic, they begin their drafts. As children begin to draft, they must come to accept the idea that writing is not permanent; it is temporary, constantly changing. Experienced writers know that drafts are only a beginning, and they understand that change will come later as their writing takes shape and meaning. The lack of interactive communication related to change and constancy in homes of poverty, however, is such that children's temporal orientation is affected. Therefore, many children view their draft as their finished product. Although kindergarten and many first-grade children's drafts *are* their finished products, they begin to learn that writers draft with the full knowledge that they will return to that piece over and over again.

In late first grade through grade five, teachers at Somerville Road found a useful way to help their children see their drafts as different from their notebooks and as an ongoing project. They provided special writing project folders to each child. Once a writing project had been selected, children moved their writing into their folder. Children began their drafts on lined paper and were asked to skip lines and write only on the front. In this way, teachers laid the groundwork for revision by providing space where changes could be made. By providing a separate place to draft, revise, and edit, teachers help young writers begin to distinguish between the various phases of the writing process.

Children's drafts vary in length based on the topics selected and on individual development. At the beginning of the year, children's drafts are generally short with few details and descriptions. Because children of poverty have a different oral story structure, their drafts may leave out critical pieces of a story. The nonverbal cues they are accustomed to using in oral storytelling may inhibit the inclusion of detail in writing. As with prewriting, teachers know that demonstration, time, and practice will help children draft more effectively as they become more comfortable in the process.

REVISION

Revision is the act of "using the writing I have already done to help me see more, feel more, think more, and learn more" (Calkins 1994, p. 39). It is the process writers use to make their intended meaning clear to themselves and to their audience. The emphasis in revising is not on repairing the draft, but on finding meaning. In order to revise, writers must be able to "re-see what has already been written" (Graves 1994, p. 225). They must view their own writing with an eye of a reader.

According to Don Graves (1994), revision follows a developmental sequence. Teachers understand the sequence and help children develop strategies they can use as they learn about revision. Young children, four- and five-year-olds, have difficulty seeing outside of themselves. To view their writing from the eyes of an audience is difficult at best and impossible at worst. Yet, teachers can assist children in beginning to think about revision. Adding on is the first step. Teachers ask questions, "Can you tell me more?" "Can you add some more detail?" When children select topics they know a great deal about, adding more information becomes easier. Teachers help children of poverty recognize their lives as meaningful. They help children acknowledge the many stories they have to tell. And, they accept and applaud children's attempts at uncovering the richness of their lives. In turn, children write much more willingly about the things *they* know rather than the things they think the *teacher* wants them to write.

The second stage of revision is perhaps the most important one, one that many teachers fail to instill. It is discovering the temporal nature of writing. Writing is not permanent; it is constantly changing in order to meet the needs of the writer and her audience. All children struggle with revision, but for children of poverty, the finality of putting something on paper is especially poignant. They see writing as having a distinct beginning and a distinct ending. The idea that writing is constantly evolving in order to communicate meaning to others is difficult to grasp. Because of children's lack of experience in meaning-making interactions with significant texts, they resist any kind of change in their writing. Teachers work with patience and consistency to help their children see the importance of revision. They begin by modeling with their own writing. Ginger Wood uses her writing to demonstrate the nature of revision. After selecting a piece from her writer's notebook, Ginger uses webbing as a prewriting strategy. She then drafts her piece on chart paper and reads it to her third graders. As she thinks aloud, she asks herself questions about her writing and about her audience. Ginger and her children discuss the process and make charts that list the possible statements and questions writers raise as they revise. Copies of the charts are placed in children's writing project folder for later use.

When Ginger first began this process of demonstration, she was excited about how well her third graders caught on and how much they assisted her in adding information, changing sentences, and taking out unnecessary information. She became frustrated, however, when children were asked to do this in their own pieces of writing. She quickly learned that just because children are willing to help others revise their writing does not mean that they are ready to revise their own. Ginger came to understand that revision is perhaps the hardest part of writing for children. She realized that the same lesson had to be done over and over again throughout the year. It took many of her children all year to begin the internalization process of revision. But, with time, she believes that the majority of her students will come to understand the temporal nature of writing.

Once children grasp the fact that writing is not permanent, the remaining stages of revision come more easily. When children recognize the need for more information, they make insertions throughout their writing, not just at the end. They recognize the main idea they are trying to convey to an audience and work to make that idea clearer. And, finally, they regard information as flexible.

Shakira, a third grader who resisted revision all year, eventually came to understand the need for it. She still didn't like to revise but she understood its purpose. "Revising means going back and reading what you have already written and then making changes if you need to. Sometimes if I put something down and don't tell the reader what it's all about, I need to revise–change it, so the reader will understand my message."

EDITING

The final phase of the writing process before publication is editing. Writers edit their work in order to "get it ready for company" (Bomer 2004); writers clean up a revised piece of writing. Children edit by focusing on spelling, mechanics, and grammar. Teachers use Nancie Atwell's (1998) idea of the contract made between writers and readers. Readers need "conventionality: for a writer to hold up his end of the bargain. As readers we count on writers to follow rules and forms so we can act as readers" (185). Like Atwell, teachers explain to children that in order for writers to be taken seriously and viewed as intelligent, mature people, then the writing they do must be conventional.

Editing for the conventions of writing should be viewed according to age appropriateness. Kindergarteners and first graders may not edit for every misspelled word, every incomplete sentence, or every period or question mark. They are still exploring and experimenting with letters and sounds, words and structure. Fifth graders, on the other hand, edit for more conventions. All children edit based on an editing checklist established in their individual classrooms. As teachers expose different conventions to their students, the editing checklist grows. So, although editing is age-dependent, all children do the work of writers by focusing on the conventions of writing.

In order to clearly convey the powerful messages young writers want to communicate, they need to understand the writing process. For all young writers, learning how to use the process is long and tedious. For writers from homes of poverty in particular, the internalization of the process requires more time than with other children. They need to spend time learning that their lives are valuable and worthy. They then need to spend time in sharing their meaningful lives with others. Once children are comfortable with the stories they have to tell and recognize the process as beneficial to the sharing of meaning, the specific techniques and strategies writers use become more important.

Writing Instruction

In addition to focusing on the meaning of writing and understanding the process writers use, teachers must also acknowledge the strategies and techniques experienced writers use. Effective writing emerges and grows as young writers engage in the work of more experienced writers. For this to occur, writing instruction must be viewed differently from what is traditionally seen in elementary schools across the country. Particularly for children whose language structures are different from the mainstream, literacy instruction must change. Teachers can no longer rely on stilted textbooks and workbooks that do not take children's unique knowledge into consideration. Teachers can no longer follow the scope and sequence of an English textbook and expect children of poverty to become writers with a sense of purpose and power. Teachers can no longer teach grammar and mechanics, spelling and punctuation, away from what is real and meaningful to children's writing. Teachers can no longer dole out traditional mainstream story starters and prompts and expect to honor the voices of children of poverty.

As was discussed in Chapter One, teachers who view writing instruction differently must accept certain principles. They must engage children in authentic time on task. Children spend concentrated time and effort on writing for real purposes and real audiences. Teachers expect children to write and they expect them to succeed. They accept approximations. They recognize that every child develops in individually unique ways and time. And they celebrate growth as it occurs. Teachers incorporate the rich language backgrounds of their children. They recognize and honor the language diversity that all children bring with them to school and they demonstrate how the language of home can be incorporated into the language of school. Last, teachers respond supportively and quickly to the writing attempts of their children. They know that the most important thing about writing is communicating meaning. Therefore, teachers let children know that their messages have been heard.

When teachers accept writing as a process of making meaning, instruction takes on a new purpose—to help children communicate to an audience. Teachers know that in order to communicate effectively, children must be engaged in writing every day. They must focus on the message to be communicated, but teachers also know that the message must be communicated in ways that are clearly understood to others. A workshop approach is used to engage children in the work of writers. Although daily writing is beneficial, writing alone will not improve the quality of the message. There must also be demonstration and instruction. It is through focus lessons that teachers instruct children in the work that writers do—strategies and techniques experienced writers use as they mold and shape their writing. Generally, focus lessons occur at the beginning of the workshop time. Lessons are designed by the teacher but directed to the specific strategies and techniques the children need. Lessons may involve strategies experienced writers use as they write or they may focus on specific techniques of using conventions. Whatever the lesson, the major purpose of instruction is to help children embrace the strategies and techniques experienced writers use in order to communicate their messages to others.

STRATEGIES

Strategies are helpful hints and general plans of action that experienced writers use as they rehearse, prewrite, draft, revise, and edit. What comes naturally to experienced writers does not always come easily to young writers. The specific strategies experienced writers use are often so imbedded in their mind that it is difficult to identify what they do at each stage of the process. Yet, for young writers to be successful, teachers must externalize these strategies. For children of poverty, in particular, it is important to clearly delineate specific strategies they can use within each stage of the process. This gives children a repertoire of strategies that can be used in any circumstance of writing.

Teachers know that the best teachers of writing are writers themselves, so they use favorite authors to teach inexperienced writers about strategies. Through author studies, children learn about the various ways authors rehearse, draft, and revise. They come to know writers as people who struggle and have devised easy ways for themselves to think about different phases of writing. Teachers rely on these authors to teach children about writing. Through the study of authors, the teachers at Somerville Road devised strategies concerning writing. They found these to be useful in helping their children internalize the phases of the writing process as well as in selecting a writing project (see Figure 5-4).

Strategies to Use While Writing

Strategies are helpful hints and general plans of action that writers use as they rehearse, draft, revise, and edit.

When rehearsing, I . . .

❏ close my eyes and think about my topic before I write
❏ keep my writer's notebook with me wherever I go
❏ jot down what I see and hear
❏ experiment with sounds and words
❏ try something new I have heard or read about

When drafting, I . . .

❏ write as quickly as I can
❏ reread my writing to keep my memories fresh
❏ try out a new technique I have learned
❏ ask myself, "Is there anything more I can say?"
❏ ask myself, "Have I included everything I need?"

When revising, I . . .

❏ reread my piece and ask, "Does this make sense?"
❏ think about my audience and what they might need
❏ add or take away to meet my audience's needs
❏ ask myself, "Does this make sense?"
❏ look for places I can rearrange
❏ think about what I'm really trying to say

When editing, I . . .

❏ use my checklist to guide my editing
❏ have a friend read my piece, looking for mistakes
❏ ask myself, "Have I spelled all my words correctly?"
❏ ask myself, "Have I shown respect for my audience?"

FIGURE 5-4.

TECHNIQUES

Techniques involve the specific ways authors use the conventions of writing to craft their messages. Traditionally, during the first few weeks of school, teachers focus their English instruction on sentences—complete and incomplete, types, sentence fragments, run-on sentences. They then move on to parts of speech—nouns (common and proper, singular and plural), verbs, adjectives, and so on. Each year beginning in second grade, English textbooks begin in the exact same way. Teachers teach the exact same things in the exact same way each year and yet, by the end of fifth grade the majority of children can neither write better nor speak better. Teaching grammar and mechanics in isolation has not worked in the past, nor will it work in the future. Do children need to know about complete sentences and nouns and verbs? Of course they do! But in order for powerful messages to be conveyed to authentic purposeful audiences, children must go further than identification. They must learn how to use these important conventions to do the work of writers.

Audience becomes of the utmost importance at this time. Without an authentic audience that is meaningful to children, learning the techniques of writing will never be useful. By providing authentic audiences, children see purpose and meaning for what they do. Teachers recognize the burdens that children face in homes of poverty. They acknowledge the hardships and know that daily living weighs heavily on children's minds. Therefore, teachers strive to give children a sense of purpose for writing that makes sense to them in their world. Effective teachers look outside of their middle-class beliefs and examine the world their children come from. They step out of their comfort zone into a world where children reside. They recognize that writing poems about my summer vacation or stories about the first time I played in the snow or the day I fell off my bicycle does not capitalize on the lives of children coming from poverty. It does not warrant a real purpose for writing in the lives of children. In fact it is this inauthentic writing that actually disempowers children (Bomer and Bomer 2001). To help children of poverty view their lives as purposeful and worthwhile, to empower them to look at problems with possible solutions, and to teach them that writing can transform their lives, teachers must provide authenticity to writing. It is only then that children will find value in the conventions of writing.

Children learn about techniques of using conventions through the books they read. They learn how authors use conventions to make their messages clearer and their writing more powerful. They come to see how Patricia MacLachlan uses powerfully vivid verbs in *All the Places to Love.* She doesn't just say the sheep *ran* away, she shows the reader that "the sheep *scattered*." Children recognize from Lester Laminack in *Saturdays and Teacakes* that he rode his bicycle up the steep hill to his grandmother's house, not through direct telling but rather through the use of the word structure, *"pedal . . . pedal . . . p-e-d-a-a-a-l-l-l."* Children talk about why Mem Fox uses periods and question marks and why Patricia Polacco uses dialogue. They discover that authors use the word *and* for emphasis as well as to connect words. And they learn that strong words help send powerful messages to their readers.

Learning how to use the techniques of writing becomes invaluable to children as they work to convey important messages to meaningful audiences. The techniques taught depend on the work young writers are trying to do in their writing. Unfortunately, it also depends on the specific curriculum teachers are required to teach. In most areas, teachers are required to cover various conventions or skills of writing. Traditionally, they have done this through isolated skill-and-drill lessons. Once teachers have a more accurate view of writing, however, they understand that it is not within the skills that writing improves but rather in the ways writers use those skills to convey meaning. Focus lessons, therefore, easily incorporate conventions as techniques writers use to do the work of writing. Teachers then begin to focus on teaching the *writer* rather than the *writing*, thereby helping young writers use techniques that more clearly get their messages across to an audience.

The list of possible technique lessons can be quite extensive depending on the grade level taught and on individual children's needs. The list of experienced writers who can help children come to understand these techniques is also quite extensive. The following, however, is a sample of possible lessons.

◆ using varied sentences to entertain the audience (types of sentences)

◆ using unique types of sentences (complete sentences, sentence fragments)

◆ using periods in different ways (at end of sentence, ellipses)

◆ using question marks for different purposes (at end of sentence, one-word conversations)

◆ using capital letters in unique ways (proper nouns, beginning of sentence, words read with excitement)

◆ using conversation to bring reality into writing (use of dialogue, quotation marks)

◆ using dialect to convey meaning (proper English and slang)

◆ using dashes (identification and use)

◆ using similes to paint pictures (identification and use)

When children become active users of conventions to fulfill meaningful purposes, they take control of their writing. They recognize that writing is not just a skill but rather a method of conveying meaning in unique ways to others.

"I use descriptive words and similes now because people, the readers, can understand what I'm trying to say. That's what writers do—make their readers try to understand. I didn't know that before last year. I didn't know that someone might read what I wrote, except the teacher. But, now I do know that other people like my writing. And, I try to make it sound right for them" (see Figure 5–5).

February 12, 2003

Wolves

The feeling of their freshly and silky fur would amaze you. They act clever as if they were teachers, smarter than a fox. That's what I would say. They snarl and and growl like a panther stalking its prey. They teeth show like light and pound into their meat with outrages power. They run as if they are gliding, moving swift and quick through the woods. They eyes are usually blue or gray. When it's blue it is the shade of a swimming pool with lots of clorean. But, When it's gray it's the shade of a thunder clouds fierce and protective. Then when it's night they growl out of their dens and cry to the moon. Wolves!

FIGURE 5-5. *"Wolves" by Connor*

6

Wandering and Wondering

As the little girl, Jenny, approached the wise woman asking all sorts of questions, the wise woman laughed and said, "My dear child, you have found the secret . . . you see, the secret of wisdom is to be curious—to take the time to look closely, to use all your senses to see and touch and taste and smell and hear. To keep on wandering and wondering. And if you don't find all the answers, you will surely find more to marvel at in this curving, curling world that spins around and around amid the stars."

These words from Eve Merriam's book *The Wise Woman and Her Secret* reflect the thoughts and feelings of teachers at Somerville Road Elementary School as they work with their children who come from disenfranchised homes. Dot Neher and Rachel Clay know that wisdom does not come in neat packages tied with pretty ribbons as the men and women in Merriam's book wanted to believe. Brenda Taylor and Donna Quarry know that wisdom comes not in tangible answers but grows as they explore their children's world, ask questions, speculate on answers, and listen to what their children have to say and write.

Teachers working in schools of poverty strive for wisdom in their daily interactions with children. They know that easy answers are not always readily available, that the inner workings of children's thought processes are something to be discovered, and that conventional practices of evaluation will not tell them all they need to know. Teachers *wander and wonder* as children constantly reveal themselves through their writing, their speech, and their interactions with others. Teachers wander among the children as they work and play, taking note of the oral language they use and asking questions concerning its meaning. They wander around the room as children engage in writing, recording the knowledge they have about print. They wonder about the lives of their children, and they work to accommodate the similarities and differences that each child brings to the classroom. They wonder about the knowledge with which children come to school, and they seek to capitalize on their strengths rather than focus on either their real or imagined deficits. In short, teachers are curious about their children. And it is within that curiosity that wise teachers emerge.

Because of national testing, standardized teaching methodologies, and reductionist thinking, the art of wandering and wondering in order to gain wisdom about children is disappearing in today's classrooms. Although there are excellent teachers who assess effectively and use that assessment to inform their instructional plans, the vast majority are overwhelmed with meeting standards, facing accountability, and preparing for tests. Teachers continue to try to provide quality classroom environments, teach with children's strengths and needs in mind, and assess in alternative ways. Yet the growing pressure of losing jobs, closing schools, and receiving public criticism has reached such proportions that many of our best teachers are either succumbing to the demands of testing or are leaving the classroom.

quality teaching amid testing

For teachers who work with children of poverty, the standardized test movement is particularly heinous. Although teachers hold high expectations for children from disadvantaged homes, they know that they may lack the background experiences needed to do well on tests. James Popham (2001, 18) puts it aptly when he says, "A meaningful amount of what's measured by today's high-stakes tests is directly attributable *not* to what students learn in school, but to what they *bring* to school in the form of their families' socioeconomic status or the academic aptitudes they happened to inherit." Middle- to upper-class families are able to provide experiences that substantively enhance their children's abilities to do well on standardized tests; lower-income families are not. The public at large then views children as failures simply because of the homes from which they come. They view schools that accommodate these children as failures. And they view children's parents as failures.

As has been noted in previous chapters, children of poverty bring to school with them experiences unique to their lives. In many instances, however, their cultural backgrounds are neither recognized nor celebrated because they do not coincide with what is tested. The rich curriculum that would help children make the connection between home and school is replaced with content easily assessed through multiple-choice test items. Rather than developing an authentic sense of print, expanding oral language through play and drama, and realizing the transforming power of writing, children are exposed to dull, dry lessons on tasks teachers know will be on the test. This in turn "tends to deaden students' genuine interest in learning. All the excitement and intellectual vibrancy that students might encounter during a really interesting lesson is driven out by a tedious, test-fostered series of drills" (Popham 2001, 21).

In this era of high-stakes testing and accountability, what can teachers do to foster the kinds of thinking that will enhance the writing abilities of children of poverty? How can teachers hold themselves accountable for what they do and demonstrate children's growth in learning at the same time? How can wise teachers *wander* and *wonder* about their children in order to help them grow in knowledge? There are no simple, clear-cut answers. While the standardized testing movement rages on, teachers must continue to strive for wisdom. We must search for ways to *wander* and *wonder* about children and hold ourselves to the highest standard possible. We must search for wisdom as we respect children and the knowledge they bring with them to school. We must search for wisdom as we become literate in assessment techniques that help children wonder about what they are doing and why they are doing it. And we must search for wisdom as we determine what children's writing actually shows about their learning.

Assessment Literates

Although there are a great number of teachers who are wise and savvy in the ways of assessment, as a whole, we are a profession of assessment illiterates. For too long we have been content to let others dictate to us what we will do in our classrooms and how we will do it. We have become complacent when it comes to professional knowledge concerning assessment. And we have allowed ourselves to accept what we view as unchangeable. In order to combat the current state of educational testing in our schools, teachers must become knowledgeable and in turn more confident to speak out and defend the practices and assessment techniques that lead to student learning and growth. Becoming an assessment literate requires that teachers *talk the talk,* talk that is fluent, knowledgeable, and accurate. We must understand terminology and talk boldly and assertively about assessment and evaluation, alternative assessment techniques, and authentic record-keeping devices.

Authorities define assessment as a "formal attempt to determine students' status with respect to educational variables of interest" (Popham 2002, 4). It is a "process of obtaining information that is used for making decisions about students, curricula and programs, and educational policy" (Nitko 2004, 5). In short, assessment focuses on the tools teachers use to obtain the necessary information about student learning. Evaluation takes us a step further in that it is a process of using both qualitative and quantitative data to make a *value judgment* about a child's ability. Therefore, teachers utilize various assessment tools in order to help them make value judgments about children's growth in writing as well as in their abilities to write.

Becoming assessment literate requires that teachers understand that to use one assessment technique to the exclusion of all others does not give an accurate account of children's knowledge and abilities. Depending only on standardized tests, teacher-made tests, and worksheets that replicate tests does not provide the information necessary for teachers to make informed decisions about the instruction children need to become better writers. In order to make quality decisions about children's writing, multiple measures of assessment must be used. Wise teachers talk with authority about alternative means of assessment and authentic methods of record-keeping and defend their use. Wise teachers know that the more information they have regarding children's knowledge and abilities in writing, the more effectively they can plan for instruction.

Focuses of Assessment

In order to be respected as wise teachers, we must hold ourselves and our children accountable for learning. It becomes imperative, therefore, that we become very good assessors of young writers in multiple ways. As we wander and wonder, we document what we see children do as they write. It is within this documentation that assessment of growth and progress can best be seen. It is in the progress made that we gain wisdom about children's abilities to write and can thereby hold ourselves accountable.

Wise teachers view assessment in terms that allow them to wander and wonder in three primary areas of student knowledge. They use assessment to focus on students' strengths, growth, and abilities. All three areas allow teachers to more accurately plan for instruction that assists children in their learning.

Throughout this book, I have focused on acknowledging the strengths with which children of poverty come to school and celebrating the growth they make to become more accomplished writers. It is from the strengths that children possess that effort is expended, growth in learning occurs, and ability in writing increases. Focusing on strengths and growth also requires teachers to think differently about teaching, learning, and assessing. No longer do teachers focus only on the end product of writing; now they attend to the process of making meaning. As children become more comfortable with the process, the end result of writing improves. Assessment, therefore, focuses on children's background knowledge of print, their use of oral language, and their attempts to communicate to others through writing. Rather than focusing on the skills that may be lacking, teachers use assessment to document what children know, analyze the strengths they do possess, plan instruction that builds on their current knowledge, and document the growth and learning abilities as they unfold.

Teachers of kindergarten children are generally very good at observing and noting children's strengths and their growth in writing. When children enter school, their knowledge of print is more visible, making it easier to plan instruction that capitalizes on those strengths. Upper-grade teachers, however, have a more difficult time assessing what children understand and can demonstrate in their writing. Whether from outside forces or internal beliefs, teachers of older learners tend to focus on the skills that may be lacking in children's writing, thus making it more difficult to determine the strengths children have. This, in turn, causes teachers to miss out on the growth that does occur.

Effective teachers, whether they are in kindergarten or in fifth grade, intricately intertwine their teaching, learning, and assessing. Teachers know that accurately assessing children's strengths leads to instruction that better fits the needs of children, which results in greater growth in writing abilities and in learning. When teachers focus only on the missing *skills* of writing, precious time is wasted and energy is expended away from authentic writing for meaningful purposes. Assessment becomes an effort in futility; it neither tells us about children's true knowledge nor does it tell us what we need to do to help children move forward.

As teachers focus on children's strengths, growth, and learning, they find that alternative measurement tools become necessary. Alternative techniques of assessment are many and varied and can be used in multiple areas of student knowledge. Teachers make decisions concerning the type of assessment tool to use based on what they wish to know about children's writing. The following are examples of various assessment techniques that teachers use in determining strengths, growth, and learning.

ANECDOTAL NOTES

Teachers use anecdotal notes to record the strengths children exhibit as well as the growth that occurs as they engage in the work of writers. Particularly at the beginning of the year, anecdotal notes help kindergarten and first-grade teachers determine the knowledge children have about print. In upper grades, anecdotal notes help teachers understand children's knowledge about story, audience awareness, and their abilities to put thought to paper. In all grade levels, anecdotal notes help teachers discover the attitudes children have toward writing that will weigh heavily on their willingness to participate in the writing process.

Anecdotal notes are easiest when written on note cards that can be filed and examined in more detail later. Some teachers have found that keeping note cards in file boxes works well; other teachers have devised a folder system that is easy to carry around as they observe children. What is written on index cards varies among grade levels. Kindergarten teachers might watch children as they play with literacy props in centers. Missy Gann notes that Eric plays with the pots and pans as he cooks dinner for the others in the group while Cedric flips through the cookbook looking for something to cook. Jan Lowery watches Dustin Lee as he looks up numbers in the telephone book and then notes that Clarissa makes a list of letterlike forms on the grocery notepad.

In both classrooms, Missy and Jan focus on what children *are* doing rather than what they may *not* know to do. They analyze their notes from these observations and plan both small- and large-group instruction that builds on the children's knowledge. Missy's plans include playing in the kitchen center and showing Eric how to use a cookbook. She also plays with Cedric and shows him how to use the cookbook to make a grocery list.

In a large group, she focuses on the fact that writers write to communicate and that communication can be for ourselves as well as for others. Missy continues her assessment, watching for the growth she knows will take place as children continue to play and learn in authentic environments.

Focusing on strengths and watching for growth in the upper grades is more difficult because of the way in which teachers have been conditioned to view writing. Because many standardized tests focus so much on the identification of parts of speech and on editing unrelated sentences for mechanics and grammar, teachers have a tendency to view students' writing in terms of what they *do not* know about the skills. It takes time and patience to modify ways of thinking about writing and focus on what children *do* know.

Amy Mount uses anecdotal notes as she watches her fourth graders use their writer's notebooks. She is concerned at the beginning of the year with children's attitudes toward and motivation for writing. She makes note of the children who enthusiastically begin writing each day and of those who struggle. She then centers her lessons on the fact that all writers struggle from time to time and introduces authors who talk about their struggles as well as their successes. As her children become more comfortable with writing, she begins focusing on what children know about writing. She tries to overlook the mistakes her children make and focuses on what they know about what writers do. Even though many use run-on sentences and sentence fragments, Amy looks beyond the mistakes to determine that complete thoughts with subjects and predicates are already in use in many children's writing. She also recognizes that some students, like Claire and Benitha, use more complex sentence structure throughout their writing. Therefore, her initial instructional lessons focus on sentences—when writers use complete sentences, why they are necessary, and when sentence fragments or run-on sentences might be useful. She then returns to her anecdotal notes, watching as children begin growing in their abilities to use sentences.

Anecdotal notes serve as invaluable information as teachers strive for wisdom in determining the knowledge children have about writing. These notes allow teachers to question themselves and their children about the knowledge they acquire as they use print for more authentic reasons as the year progresses.

CHECKLISTS

Teachers in all grade levels use checklists to determine the knowledge children have about writing at any given time. Individual teachers design checklists based on the group of children they work with and may include processes as well as conventions of writing, or they may be designed based on state curriculum requirements or textbook lessons. The best checklists, however, are designed by teachers who know and understand the process of writing as well as how children develop as writers (see Appendix J).

Teachers use checklists to determine the extent of knowledge children have about writing and then plan lessons with that knowledge in mind. Rather than teach lessons in the sequence set out by the textbook, teachers base instructional decisions on the strengths children exhibit. Donna Quarry notices that her third graders recognize writing as a way of communicating with others, and they are eager to share each day. Creating a checklist that demonstrates these strengths enables her to focus on audience awareness and the reasons writers write. Donna then plans instruction that focuses her students' attention on who an audience might be and what types of writing are best suited. The use of conventions follows as children gain more respect for the needs of their audience.

Checklists also serve as an accountability tool for teachers and for children. As strategies and techniques of writing are taught through focus lessons, the teacher notes dates of instruction. Assessment occurs as teachers observe children's writing. Through the anecdotal notes she keeps, Mandy Brown notices that her third graders use sentences but they all follow the same pattern: they are all declarative types of sentences. Mandy's anecdotal records lead her to plan instruction to introduce children to the ways experienced writers use different types of sentences to keep their readers interested. Mandy then uses a checklist to assess children's attempts at using different types of sentences. As children continue to write, Mandy notices that only a few are experimenting with different sentence structure. Although she understands the developmental nature of children's writing and knows that different children assimilate new skills at different times, she feels it necessary to continue to provide instruction on types of sentences. So, she divides her class into two groups and conducts further focus lessons with each group based on the needs they each have. Mandy's use of checklists as assessment informs her planning and she instructs based on the needs of her children.

Checklists provide tangible evidence of children's strengths and abilities in writing. They serve as documentation of lessons taught and how well children put into practice the those lessons.

INTERVIEWS/QUESTIONNAIRES

Because teachers know that attitudes as well as knowledge play an important role in children's enthusiasm and later ability to write, they find ways to determine children's attitudes and knowledge about writing. Teachers may conduct individual or small-group interviews as well as distribute written questionnaires at the beginning of the year to determine children's attitudes toward writing. Generally, the older children are, the more negative their attitudes toward writing, particularly among children of poverty. Without knowing they have a voice, children of poverty have only viewed writing as a way for teachers to grade them on spelling, punctuation, and grammar. Their writing has had very little meaning and virtually no communicative value. Therefore, they see writing as tedious and something they cannot do well. Through interviews and questionnaires, teachers not only let children know that writing is important, they also use children's responses to plan lessons that dispel those negative attitudes and provide them meaningful reasons to write and authentic audiences to write for.

Interviews and questionnaires also allow teachers to discover the misconceptions children have concerning writing. As has been stated earlier, many children equate writing with spelling and handwriting. They believe that if they can spell accurately and handwrite neatly, they are able to write. Other children only see writing as using periods at the end of sentences and capital letters at the beginning of sentences. Again, they do not recognize the true nature of writing; it is only about getting the words right. Based on this knowledge, teachers realize that the very essence of writing—communication—has been lost. Children do not see that their words hold value or power. Instruction then begins with lessons on what writing really is. Teachers spend time with experienced writers and their books, encouraging children to question why these authors do the things they do. They talk to children about the audience writers write for, the reasons they write, and the purpose their writing serves. Although teachers may talk about mechanics, parts of speech, and word choice, the primary focus is on the purpose for which writers use these things. In this way, teachers dispel the myth that good writing equates with good spelling, good handwriting, and correct use of punctuation.

By using interviews and questionnaires at the beginning of the year as well as at the end of year, teachers and children alike are able to see the growth they made throughout the year.

SELF-ASSESSMENT

A vital component of any quality writing program is self-assessment. Particularly for children of poverty who have spent very little time looking at what they do and why they do it, self-assessment allows them to know themselves more intimately as writers. Teachers teach children to self-assess by modeling. Just as teachers externalize the process of writing for children as they learn, so teachers must externalize the types of questions one asks oneself in order to assess. Children make cue cards based on the types of questions they need to ask themselves about what they do as writers. The greater the depth of self-assessment, the greater chance children have of becoming writers.

In addition to cue cards, teachers provide self-assessment check sheets that children attach to their writing project folders. These check sheets provide a place where, once a week, children list the types of strategies and techniques they use as writers. Check sheets also provide a place where children can identify the one or two new things they have learned to do in a particular week (see Appendix K).

Goal setting is another form of self-assessment. Connie Hurst, a second-grade teacher, helps her children set goals for themselves at the beginning of each writers' workshop. Before children leave the carpet from whole-group instruction, she asks each child to verbalize his or her goal for the day. At the end of writers' workshop, she asks the children to rate themselves as to how well they accomplished their goal. Second graders find this difficult at the beginning of the year, but Connie is consistent and by the end of the first semester, all her second graders are setting goals and assessing themselves.

Self-assessment in writing leads to reflection. For children of poverty who have had limited experience with thinking about their own thinking, it provides them with a sense of accomplishment and a belief in themselves as writers with important things to say.

WRITING SAMPLES

There is nothing more powerful to demonstrate growth in learning than students' actual writing samples. Through these samples teachers assess how far children have come in their knowledge about writing and in their abilities to write. Children also see how much they have improved as they look back through their writer's notebooks as well as their writing project folders. Self-assessment increases as they make note of the strengths they possessed at the beginning of the year as well as the newfound knowledge acquired by the end of the year.

By looking at writing samples, teachers assess growth and knowledge and plan lessons that help children move forward in their writing. When

Marissa Pedings examines her fifth graders' writing project folders, she notices that the majority of her children need help in writing more detailed descriptions. She also discovers that children's use of proper nouns is limited as well. She decides to combine the two needs and plan lessons on how writers use proper nouns to make their writing more descriptive and detailed. Using the book *Missing May*, Marissa shows her children how Cynthia Rylant includes proper nouns to describe in more detail. Rylant describes May's cabinets not in general terms but descriptively with the use of brand names, "I saw *Oreos* and *Ruffles* and big bags of Snickers. I saw fat bags of marshmallows and cans of *SpaghettiO's* and a little plastic bear full of honey. There were real glass bottles of *Coke*.... And, best of all, a carton of real chocolate milk that said *Hershey's*" (8). Marissa demonstrates to her children how authors use the conventions of writing in ways that enhance writing. She knows how to plan because of the close observations she makes of her children's writing.

Teachers use writer's notebooks and writing project folders to determine the extent of growth and learning children have acquired in the writing process. By periodically examining writing project folders, teachers determine how well and to what extent children understand prewriting, drafting, and revision. In like manner, as teachers examine writer's notebooks, they gain an understanding about how children perceive the notebook, how well they use it as seedbeds for later writing, and how well they practice and experiment with techniques and conventions. Many teachers use checklists to further document what they see children doing in their writing.

Assessment is more authentic when actual writing samples are used; the true nature of children's growth and knowledge is evident.

RUBRICS

Rubrics are a form of rating scale used to evaluate children's progress toward a benchmark or standard. Teachers use rubrics to assess children's knowledge of writing in terms of how well they apply the techniques and strategies of writers. Rubrics make it possible for both children and teachers to know exactly what elements of writing matter the most. Rubrics help teachers determine how well young writers do the work of more experienced writers.

Linda D'Antonio uses rubrics with her fourth graders and Rachel Clay uses them with her fifth graders. Both teachers believe that children are an integral part of the development of rubrics; after all, it is their writing that will be assessed. In schools that serve children of poverty, teachers work extra hard to help children learn to develop rubrics. Because it requires internal thinking and self-assessment, initially children find it difficult. Teachers spend time at the beginning of the year modeling and talking through the process of rubric development. Linda uses her own writing along with the checklist she and her children create as she teaches focus lessons. She shows children how to create a rubric based on what has been taught as well as what they are doing in their writing. Prior to a writing project due date, Rachel spends time with her children determining what techniques should be included on the rubric. They examine prior lessons as well as checklists. Rachel makes sure her children understand that both the techniques of craft and conventions are important in assessing a final piece of writing (see Appendix L).

For all teachers, rubrics serve as an authentic assessment tool in determining children's knowledge of writing. They also serve as evidence of growth throughout the year as techniques and strategies are added. Children are able to determine their own growth and strengths as writers by using rubrics.

TEACHER-MADE TESTS/WORKSHEETS

Is there a place in the writers' workshop for worksheets and tests? In an ideal world where educators and the general public cared about growth in application and problem solving, the answer would be no. In the world in which we live, with the focus directed toward product, fragmented curriculum, and standardized testing, the answer is yes; there must be a place. As responsible teachers, we must take into consideration the future expectations required of our young writers in the larger world of schooling. For now, every child will take a standardized test in every grade level beginning in first grade and continuing through college. While we, as conscientious educators, continue to fight against the atrocious nature of current testing practices, we cannot simply ignore them. Thus, it becomes our responsibility to help children not only to write with meaning and power but also to understand the nature of tests and what they will be asked to do throughout their education.

There are effective ways to deal with the testing issue and there are ineffective ways. What should *not* be done is a tunnel-vision approach to teaching and assessing where everything taught is assessed through multiple-choice questions. Children learn neither how to write nor speak better when this approach is taken. What *should* be done is a continuation of assessment that informs instruction. Instruction then informs children about what matters most in their writing. And, what matters most is in turn assessed in authentic ways. Teaching in this manner allows children to grow in knowledge about writing and allows teachers to then demonstrate what that knowledge might look like on a standardized test. Children are confident in themselves as writers with important things to say and they are convinced that they can demonstrate their knowledge in multiple ways.

Dot Neher recognizes the responsibility she has to her fourth graders in both writing and in testing. She uses her children's writing to inform her instruction and then assesses their abilities to apply new knowledge in their writing. Children of poverty, in particular, have less experience in transferring information to multiple sources. Although they accomplish a great deal in using different techniques of writers, they do not easily make the transition to a new situation. Dot knows this and realizes she must be direct in helping children transfer knowledge from one format to another. Therefore, she introduces the concept of testing only after children are comfortable in their writing. After she has taught children how experienced writers use complete sentences in their writing, she has children examine their own writing for complete sentences. She then shows children what this might look like on a test. These sessions are short but direct. Her goal is to expose her children to a test-taking format, but her primary interest continues to be in children's writing.

In Marissa Pedings' fifth-grade classroom, she understands the need to periodically test her children on skills they will be expected to know on a standardized test. Like other effective teachers of writing, she focuses her instructional lessons on strategies and techniques experienced writers use. But she also includes lessons on what these strategies and techniques might sound and look like on a test. She makes a direct relationship between children's writing and questions on a test. Children take the first test together with the help of Marissa. She asks them to look at their writer's notebooks and their writing project folder along with the checklists they are keeping. With Marissa's help, children examine their writing and make lists of the specific skills they are using. The children spend time talking about the skills, why authors use them, and how they work in their writing. Marissa then demonstrates how a particular skill might look on a test. For example, children are using capital letters for various purposes—to start a sentence, to indicate a proper noun, and to show readers to read with excitement. She writes multiple-choice questions on the board and asks children to select the response that uses capital letters correctly. As the year progresses, children become accustomed to this practice and look forward to showing their knowledge in multiple ways. When test time rolls around, children are less likely to freeze or forget what they know about writing.

Testing is here to stay for the immediate future. Wise teachers of writing recognize the responsibility they have to teach children to write with passion and meaning. They also recognize the responsibility they have to prepare children for a future that includes test-taking. Effective teachers of writing find ways to incorporate test-taking skills into the natural course of instruction. They find ways to help children show their knowledge of writing in multiple ways.

Conclusion

Assessment in today's classroom requires an understanding about alternative ways to recognize the strengths, growth, and abilities of children and their writing. It requires that teachers reexamine their own personal beliefs about the connections between and among assessment, instruction, and learning. It requires that teachers *wander* and *wonder* as children write for meaning and purpose. It also requires that children become self-assessors as they strive to demonstrate what they actually know about writing. And it requires that administrators support and encourage the use of alternative assessment techniques in holding teachers and children accountable.

Wisdom about strengths, growth, and abilities comes as teachers *wander and wonder* through children's writing lives. It comes as teachers question themselves and their children. It comes as teachers seek answers that make sense in the context of children's writing. It comes as teachers honor the lives and listen to the voices of their children.

Teachers who heed the words of the wise woman return to their classrooms in good time, "and they, like Jenny, saunter and sing, taste and touch, and listen and laugh and cry" and they, too, grow up to become wise teachers themselves.

Appendix A: Directions for Flip Book

Start with three sheets of paper (paper is patterned for demonstration only).

Stack as shown below:

Fold on the dotted line:

Staple at folded edge to finish.

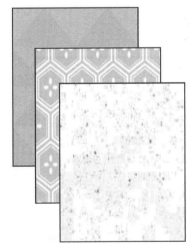  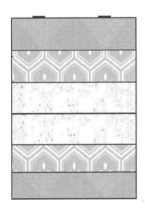

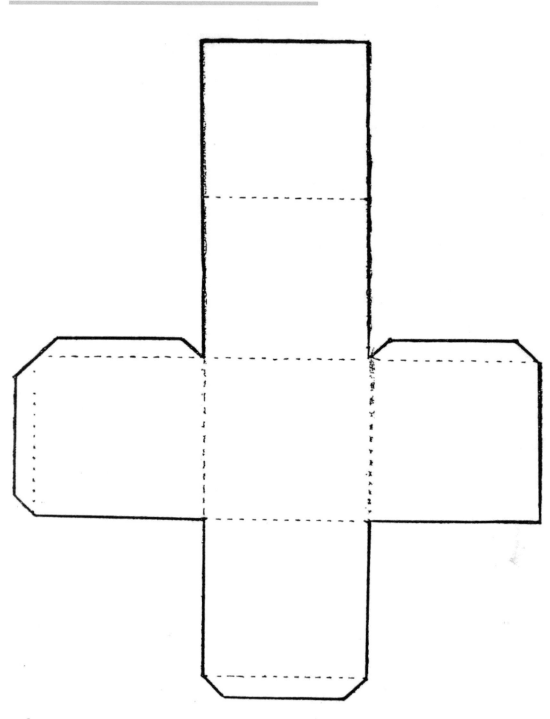

Appendix C: Books That Build Community and Encourage Critical Thinking

ALIKI. 1984. *Feelings.* New York: Harper Trophy.

BAYLOR, BYRD. 1995. *I'm in Charge of Celebrations.* New York: Aladdin.

BUNTING, EVE. 1991. *Fly Away Home.* New York: Clarion.

———. 1994. *Smokey Nights.* San Diego, CA: Harcourt Brace.

———. 1996. *Train to Somewhere.* New York: Clarion.

CANNON, JANELL. 1997. *Stellaluna.* San Diego, CA: Harcourt Brace.

CARLSON, NANCY. 1988. *I Like Me.* New York: Penguin Group.

———. 1997. *ABC I Like Me.* New York: Puffin Books.

DE PAOLA, TOMIE. 1989. *The Art Lesson.* New York: G. P. Putnam's Sons.

DEREGNIERS, BEATRICE. 1988. *The Way I Feel Sometimes.* New York: Clarion Books.

DORROS, ARTHUR. 1991. *Abuela.* New York: Dutton's Children's Books.

ESTES, ELINOR. 1944. *100 Dresses.* New York: Harcourt.

FLOUNOY, VALERIE. 1985. *Patchwork Quilt.* New York: Dial Books.

FOX, MEM. 1985. *Wilford Gordon McDonald Partridge.* Brooklyn, NY: Kane/Miller Publishers.

———. 1989. *Feathers and Fools.* Orlando, FL: Harcourt.

———. 1989. *Sophie.* Orlando, FL: Harcourt.

———. 1994. *Tough Boris.* San Diego, CA: Harcourt, Brace, Jovanovich.

———. 1997. *Whoever You Are.* Orlando, FL: Harcourt Brace.

GREENFIELD, ELOISE. 1988. *Grandpa's Face.* Philomel Books.

HENKES, KEVIN. 1991. *Chrysanthemum.* New York: Harper Trophy.

HUFFMAN, MARY. 1991. *Amazing Grace.* New York: Scholastic.

KING, MARGAREE. 1993. *Uncle Jed's Barbershop.* New York: Simon and Schuster.

MADRIGAL, ANTONIO HERNANDEZ. 1999. *Erandi's Braids.* New York: Putnam's.

MCKISSACK, PATRICIA. 2001. *Goin' Someplace Special.* New York: Simon and Schuster.

PFISTER, MARCUS. 1992. *Rainbow Fish.* New York: Scholastic.

POLACCO, PATRICIA. 1998. *Thank You, Mr. Falker.* New York: Philomel.

RATHMANN, PEGGY. 1991. *Ruby the Copy Cat.* New York: Scholastic.

RYLANT, CYNTHIA. 1985. *The Relatives Came.* New York: Bradbury Press.

SHANNON, DAVID. 1998. *A Bad Case of the Stripes.* New York: Blue Sky Press.

WOODSON, JACQUELINE. 1998. *We Had a Picnic Last Sunday Past.* New York: Hyperion.

———. 2001. *The Other Side.* New York: Putnam's Sons.

YEP, LAURENCE. 1991. *The Star Fisher.* New York: Puffin Books.

In order to build acceptance, respect, and tolerance, books are read and discussed at the beginning of the year. Teachers plan extension experiences based on the books. Possible extensions might be:

- Small-group grand conversations
- Role play/simulation
- Readers' theater
- Story retelling
- Puppet dramatization
- Letters to the author
- Ending rewrites

Appendix D: Cultural Fairy Tales, Fables, and Folktales

AFRICAN AMERICAN FAIRY/FOLKTALES

ALEXANDER, LLOYD. 1992. *The Fortune Tellers.* New York: Dutton's Children's Books.

ALLEN, DEBBIE, AND KADIR NELSON. 1999. *Brothers of the Knight.* New York: Dial Books.

AMIN, KARIMA. 1999. *Adventures of Brer Rabbit.* Orlando, FL: Family Learning.

HAMILTON, VIRGINIA. 1993. *The People Could Fly.* New York: Blue Sky Press.

——. 1995. *Her Stories: African American Folktales.* New York: Blue Sky Press.

——. 2000. *The Girl Who Spun Gold.* New York: Blue Sky Press.

——. 2004. *Wee Winnie Witch's Skinny.* New York: Blue Sky Press.

LESTER, JULIUS. 1994. *John Henry.* New York: Dial Books.

MCKISSACK, PATRICIA. 1986. *Flossie and the Fox.* New York: Dial Books.

——. 1988. *Mirandy and Brother Wind.* New York: Dial Books.

MENDEZ, PHIL. 1989. *The Black Snowman.* New York: Scholastic.

NOLEN, JERDINE. 2000. *Big Jabe. New York*: Lothrop, Lee, and Shepard Books.

——. 2003. *Thunder Rose.* San Diego, CA: Harcourt.

RINGGOLD, FAITH. 1999. *The Invisible Princess.* New York: Dragonfly Books.

ROSALES, MELODYE. 1999. *Leola and Honeybears.* New York: Scholastic.

SAN SOUCI, ROBERT D. 1992. *Sukey and the Mermaid.* New York: Four Winds Press.

——. 1995. *The Faithful Friend.* New York: Simon and Schuster.

SEEGER, PETE. 1986. *Abiyoyo.* New York: Aladdin.

ASIAN FAIRY/FOLKTALES

AI-LING, LOUIE. 1983. *Yeh-Shen: A Cinderella Story.* New York: Puffin Books.

BISHOP, CLAIR. 1938. *The Five Chinese Brothers.* New York: Coward, McCann, and Geoghegan.

CLIMO, SHIRLEY. 1993. *The Korean Cinderella.* New York: Harper Collins.

DEMI. 1980. *Liang and the Magic Paintbrush.* New York: Henry Holt.

——. 1990. *The Empty Pot.* New York: Henry Holt.

——. 1997. *One Grain of Rice.* New York: Scholastic.

HONG, LILY TOY. 1995. *The Empress and the Silkworm.* Morton Grove, IL: Albert Whitman.

LIN, GRACE & KATHY TUCKER. 2003. *The Seven Chinese Sisters.* Morton Grove, IL: Albert Whitman.

MOSEL, ARLENE. 1968. *Tikki Tikki Tembo.* New York: Holt, Rinehart, Winston.

YEP, LAURENCE. 1985. *Dragon Steel.* New York: Harper and Row.

YOUNG, ED. 1989. *Lon Po Po.* New York: Scholastic.

Hispanic Fairy/Folktales

Baca, Ana. 1999. *Chiles for Benito.* Houston, TX: Pinata Books.

Boada, Francesca. 2001. *Cinderella.* San Francisco, CA: Chronicle Books.

de Paola, Tomie. 2002. Adelita: *A Mexican Cinderella Story.* New York: G. P. Putnam's Sons.

Ehlert, Lois. 1997. *Cuckoo: A Mexican Folktale.* New York: Harcourt Brace.

Fisher, Leonard E. 1988. *Pyramid of the Sun: Pyramid of the Moon.* New York: Macmillan.

Garcia, Guy. 1995. *Spirit of the Maya.* New York: Walker Books.

Gerson, Mary-Joan, and Maya Gonzalez. 2001. *Fiesta Femenina: Celebrating Women in Mexican Folktales.* New York: Barefoot Books.

Gonzalez, Lucia. 1997. *Senor Cat's Romance and Other Favorite Stories from Latin America.* New York: Scholastic.

Hayes, Joe. 1987. *La Llorona, The Weeping Woman.* Dexter, MI: Thomson-Shore.

Mora, Pat. 2000. *The Night the Moon Fell.* Toronto, Ontario: Groundwood Books.

———. 2001. *The Race of Toad and Deer.* Toronto, Ontario: Groundwood Books.

Pijoan, Teresa. 1996. *Listen, A Story Comes.* Santa Fe, NM: Red Crane Books.

San Souci, Robert D. 2000. *Little Gold Star: A Spanish American Cinderella Tale.* New York: HarperCollins.

Appendix E: Patterned Books

CARLE, ERIC. 1969. *The Very Hungry Caterpillar.* New York: Philomel.

——. 1983. *Brown Bear, Brown Bear.* New York: Holt, Rinehart, Winston.

——. 1991. *Polar Bear, Polar Bear.* New York: Scholastic.

COWLEY, JOY. 1990. *A Monster Sandwich.* Bothell, WA: Wright Group.

NUMEROFF, LAURA. 1985. *If You Give a Mouse a Cookie.* New York: HarperCollins.

——. 1991. *If You Give a Moose a Muffin.* New York: HarperCollins.

——. 1998. *If You Give a Pig a Pancake.* New York: HarperCollins.

SHANNON, DAVID. 1998. *No, David.* New York: Scholastic.

WILLIAMS, SUE. 1989. *I Went Walking.* New York: Red Wagon Books.

Appendix F: Poetry

DUNNING, STEPHEN, EDWARD LEUDERS, AND HUGH SMITH. 1966. *Reflections on a Gift of Watermelon Pickle.* New York: Scholastic.

FLEISCHMAN, PAUL. 1988. *Joyful Noise: Poems for Two Voices.* New York: Trumpet.

FROST, ROBERT. 1975. *You Come Too.* New York: Scholastic.

GIOVANNI, NIKKI. 1985. *Spin a Soft Black Song.* New York: Trumpet.

———. 1993. *Ego-Tripping and Other Poems.* Brooklyn, NY: Lawrence Hill Books.

GREENFIELD, ELOISE. 1978. *Honey, I Love and Other Love Poems.* New York: Trumpet.

HEARD, GEORGIA. 2002. *This Place I Know: Poems of Comfort (Selected by Heard).* Cambridge, MA: Candlewick Press.

HOBERMAN, MARY ANN. 1991. *Fathers, Mothers, Sisters, Brothers: A Collection of Family Poems.* New York: Little Brown.

HUDSON, WADE. 1993. *Pass It On: African-American Poetry for Children (Selected by Hudson).* New York: Scholastic.

HUGHES, LANGSTON. 1994. *The Dream Keeper and Other Poems.* New York: Scholastic.

LEWIS, J. PATRICK. 1998. *Doodle Dandies: Poems That Take Shape.* New York: Scholastic.

MORA, PAT. 1999. *My Own True Name: New and Selected Poems for Young Adults.* Houston, TX: Pinata Books.

MOSS, JEFF. 1997. *Bone Poems.* New York: Scholastic.

PRELUTSKY, JACK. 1993. *It's Raining Pigs and Noodles.* New York: HarperCollins.

ROGASKY, BARBARA. 1994. *Winter Poems (Selected by Rogasky).* New York: Scholastic.

SANCHEZ, SONIA. 1971. *It's a New Day: Poems for Young Brothas and Sistuhs.* New York: Broadside Press.

SILVERSTEIN, SHEL. 1974. *Where the Sidewalk Ends.* New York: HarperCollins.

SOTO, GARY. 1992. *Neighborhood Odes.* New York: Scholastic.

SPINELLI, EILEEN. 1998. *When Mama Comes Home Tonight.* New York: Scholastic.

THOMAS, JOYCE C. 1993. *Brown Honey in Broomwheat Tea.* New York: Harper/Trophy.

YOLEN, JANE. 2000. *Street Rhymes Around the World.* Honesdale, PA: Wordsong/Boyds Mill Press.

Appendix G: Culturally Diverse Nursery Rhymes

ADA, ALMA FLOR. 2003. *Pio Peep!* New York: HarperCollins.

CREWS, NINA. 2004. *The Neighborhood Mother Goose.* New York: Greenwillow Books.

DEFOREST, CHARLOTTE. 1968. *The Prancing Pony.* New York: Walker/Weatherhill.

DOWNS, CYNTHIA. 1996. *Hispanic Games and Rhymes.* Grand Rapids, MI: Instructional Fair.

FITZGERALD, ELLA. 2003. *A Tisket, A Tasket.* New York: Philomel.

GRIEGO, MARGOT C. ET AL. 1988. *Tortillitas para mamá.* New York: Henry Holt.

GRIMES, NIKKI. 1993. *From a Child's Heart.* New York: Just Us Books.

HUDSON, CHERYL WILLIS. 1997. *Many Colors of Mother Goose.* East Orange, NJ: Just Us Books.

JARAMILLO, N. P. 1996. *Grandmother's Nursery Rhymes.* New York: Holt.

KROLL, VIRGINIA. 1995. *Jaha and Jamil Went Down the Hill.* Santa Fe, NM: Charlesburg Publishers.

MERRIAM, EVE. 1996. *Inner City Mother Goose.* New York: Simon and Schuster.

MOSES, WILL. 2003. *Will Moses' Mother Goose.* New York: Philomel.

POLACCO, PATRICIA. 1995. *Babushka's Mother Goose.* New York: Philomel.

SCHON, ISABEL. 1983. *Dona Blanca & Other Hispanic Nursery Rhymes and Games.* Minneapolis, MN: T. S. Denison.

WASHINGTON, MICHELLE. 2001. *A Treasury of African American ABC's and Nursery Rhymes for Children.* New York: Arthorhouse.

YOUNG, ED. 1968. *Chinese Mother Goose.* Cleveland, OH: World Publishing Co.

Appendix H: Books About Families

BUNTING, EVE. 1994. *Smokey Nights.* San Diego, CA: Harcourt Brace.

——. 1996. *Train to Somewhere.* New York: Clarion.

DORROS, ARTHUR. 1991. *Abuela.* New York: Dutton's Children's Books.

FLOUNOY, VALERIE. 1985. *The Patchwork Quilt.* Orlando FL: Harcourt.

LAMINACK, LESTER. 2004. *Saturdays and Teacakes.* Atlanta, GA: Peachtree.

MITCHELL, MARGAREE KING. 1993. *Uncle Jed's Barbershop.* New York: Simon and Schuster.

NOLAN, JERDINE. 1999. *In My Mama's Kitchen.* New York: HarperCollins.

POLACCO, PATRICIA. 1994. *My Rotten Red-Headed Older Brother.* New York: Philomel.

——. 1995. *My Ol' Man.* New York: Philomel.

WOODSON, JACQUELINE. 1998. *We Had a Picnic This Sunday Past.* New York: Hyperion.

——. 2000. *Sweet, Sweet Memory.* New York: Hyperion.

——. 2001. *The Other Side.* New York: Putnam's Sons.

——. 2002. *Our Gracie Aunt.* New York: Hyperion.

——. 2002. *Visiting Day.* New York: Scholastic.

WORDLESS PICTURE BOOKS

BANG, MOLLY. 1980. *The Grey Lady and the Strawberry Snatcher.* New York: Four Winds Press.

CARLE, ERIC. 1971. *Do You Want to Be My Friend?* New York: Harper Collins.

——. 1996. *I See a Song.* New York: Scholastic.

DE PAOLA, TOMIE. 1981. *The Hunter and the Animals.* New York: Holiday House.

FLEISCHMAN, PAUL. 2004. *Sidewalk Circus.* New York: Candlewick Press.

JENKINS, STEVE. 2003. *Looking Down.* Boston, MA: Houghton Mifflin.

MAYER, MERCER. 1967. *A Boy, A Dog, and a Frog.* New York: Dial Books for Young Readers.

TURKLE, BRINTON. 1992. *Deep in the Forest.* New York: Puffin Books.

BOOKS WITH FEW WORDS

CARLE, ERIC. 1983. *Brown Bear, Brown Bear.* New York: Holt, Rinehart, Winston.

——. 1991. *Polar Bear, Polar Bear.* New York: Scholastic.

——. 1993. *Today Is Monday.* New York: Scholastic.

FLEMING, DENISE. 1991. *In the Tall Tall Grass.* New York: Henry Holt.

FOX, MEM. 1994. *Tough Boris.* San Diego, CA: Harcourt, Brace, Jovanovich.

MARTIN, BILL JR. 1994. *The Maestro Plays.* New York: Holt, Rinehart, and Winston.

SHANNON, DAVID. 1998. *No, David.* New York: Scholastic.

BOOKS THAT ASK QUESTIONS

ASCH, FRANK. 2000. *The Sun Is My Favorite Star.* New York: Harcourt.

CARLE, ERIC. 1999. *Papa, Please Get the Moon for Me.* New York: Simon and Schuster.

FOX, MEM. 1995. *Guess What?* New York: Harcourt Brace.

GUARINO, DEBORAH. 1997. *Is Your Mama a Llama?* New York: Scholastic.

BOOKS THAT LABEL

SCARRY, RICHARD. 1974. *Cars and Trucks and Things That Go.* Crawfordsville, IN: Golden Books.

——. 1980. *Best Word Book Ever.* Crawfordsville, IN: Golden Books.

ABC BOOKS

BASE, GRAEME. 1986. *Animalia.* New York: Harry Abrams.

CLINE-RANSOM, LESA. 2001. *Quilt Alphabet.* New York: Holiday House.

HEPWORTH, CATHI. 1992. *Antics!* New York: Trumpet.

LOBEL, ARNOLD. 1981. *On Market Street.* New York: Scholastic.

MERRIAM, EVE. 1987. *Halloween ABC.* New York: Trumpet.

PALLOTTA, JERRY. 1989. *The Yucky Reptile Alphabet Book.* New York: Trumpet.

——. 1991. *The Underwater Alphabet Book.* New York: Trumpet.

——. 1993. *The Extinct Alphabet Book.* New York: Trumpet.

PELLETIER, DAVID. 1996. *The Graphic Alphabet.* New York: Scholastic.

TOBIAS, TOBI. 1998. *A World of Words: An ABC of Quotations.* New York: Lothrop, Lee and Shepard Books.

VIORST, JUDITH. 1994. *The Alphabet from A to Z.* New York: Atheneum.

BOOKS IN THE FORM OF LETTERS

CLEARY, BEVERLY. 1983. *Dear Mr. Henshaw.* New York: HarperCollins.

GRAY, LIBBA MOORE. 1993. *Dear Willie Rudd,.* New York: Simon and Schuster.

JAMES, SIMON. 1991. *Dear Mr. Blueberry.* New York: Simon and Schuster.

STEWART, MARY. 1997. *The Gardener.* New York: Farrar, Straus, Giroux.

AFRICAN AMERICAN STORIES/NARRATIVES

BOYD, CANDY DAWSON. 1993. *Chevrolet Saturdays.* New York: MacMillan.

BRADBY, MARIE. 1995. *The Longest Wait.* New York: Orchard Books.

——. 1995. *More Than Anything Else.* New York: Orchard Books.

BUNTING, EVE. 1994. *Flower Garden.* New York: Harcourt Brace Jovanovich.

——. 1994. *Smokey Nights.* New York: San Diego, CA: Harcourt.

COWLEY, JOY. 1997. *Singing Down the Rain.* New York: HarperCollins.

CREWS, DONALD. 1991. *Big Mama's.* New York: Greenwillow Books.

CURTIS, CHRISTOPHER PAUL. 1995. *The Watsons Go to Birmingham.* New York: Delacorte Press.

——. 1999. *Bud, Not Buddy.* New York: Delacorte Press.

EISENBURG, PHYLLIS ROSE. 1995. *You're My Nikki.* New York: Puffin Books.

FIELDS, JULIA. 1988. *The Green Lion on Zion Street.* New York: McElderry Books.

FLOURNOY, VALERIA. 1985. *The Patchwork Quilt.* New York: Dial Books.

GRAY, LIBBA MOORE. 1993. *Dear Willie Rudd,.* New York: Simon and Schuster.

GREENFIELD, ELOISE. 1977. *Africa Dream.* New York: Harper Trophy.

——. 1988. *Grandpa's Face.* New York: Philomel Books.

——. 1988. *Nathaniel Talking.* New York: Black Butterfly.

——. 1991. *Night on Neighborhood Street.* New York: Dial Books.

HOFFMAN, MARY. 1991. *Amazing Grace.* New York: Scholastic.

——. 1995. *Boundless Grace.* New York: Scholastic.

ISADORA, RACHEL. 1979. *Ben's Trumpet.* New York: Greenwillow Books.

KEATS, EZRA JACK. 1962. *Snowy Day.* New York: Viking Press.

——. 1964. *Whistle for Willie.* New York: Penguin Group.

MCKISSACK, PATRICIA. 1999. *Nettie Jo's Friends.* New York: Econo-Clad Books.

——. 2001. *Goin Someplace Special.* New York: Simon and Schuster.

MILLER, WILLIAM. 2001. *Zora Hurston and the Chinaberry Tree.* New York: Lee and Low Books.

——. 2002. *Night Golf.* New York: Lee and Low Books.

MITCHELL, MARGAREE KING. 1993. *Uncle Jed's Barbershop.* New York: Simon and Schuster.

NOLEN, JERDINE. 1999. *In My Mama's Kitchen.* New York: HarperCollins.

O'DELL, SCOTT. 1989. *My Name Is Not Angelica.* Boston, MA: Houghton Mifflin.

PILKEY, DAVE. 1996. *The Paperboy.* New York: Orchard Books.

PINKNEY, ANDREA DAVIS. 1998. *Duke Ellington.* New York: Hyperion Books.

RAPPAPORT, DOREEN. 2001. *Martin's Big Words.* New York: Hyperion Books.

RINGGOLD, FAITH. 1991. *Tar Beach.* New York: Scholastic.

SMOTHERS, ETHEL. 2001. *Auntee Edna.* Grand Rapids, MI: Eerdman's Books.

STOLZ, MARY. 1988. *Storm in the Night.* New York: Harper Trophy.

WOODSON, JACQUELINE. 1994. *I Hadn't Meant to Tell You This.* New York: Delacorte Books.

——. 1998. *We Had a Picnic Last Sunday Past.* New York: Hyperion.

——. 2001. *The Other Side.* New York: Putnam's.

YOLEN, JANE. 1997. *Miz Berlin Walks.* New York: Philomel Books.

ASIAN STORIES/NARRATIVES

CHIN, STEVEN. 1992. *When Justice Failed: The Fred Korematsu Story.* New York: Steck-Vaughn.

CHOI, SOOK NYUL. 1991. *Year of Impossible Goodbyes.* Boston, MA: Houghton Mifflin.

——. 1993. *Echoes of the White Giraffe.* Boston, MA: Houghton Mifflin.

COERR, ELEANOR. 1997. *Sadako and the Thousand Paper Cranes.* New York: Putnam.

MOCHIZUKI, KEN. 1993. *Baseball Saved Us.* New York: Scholastic.

PARK, LINDA SUE. 2000. *The Kite Fighters.* New York: Clarion Books.

PULLMAN, PHILIP. 2000. *The Firework-Maker's Daughter.* New York: Scholastic.

SAY, ALLEN. 1991. *Tree of Cranes.* Boston, MA: Houghton Mifflin.

———. 1993. *Grandfather's Journey.* Boston, MA: Houghton Mifflin.

UCHIDA, YOSHIKO. 1981. *A Jar of Dreams.* New York: Simon and Schuster.

YEP, LAURENCE. 1991. *The Star Fisher.* New York: Penguin Books.

———. 1995. *Thief of Hearts.* New York: HarperCollins

HISPANIC STORIES/NARRATIVES

ARMAS, TERESA. 2003. *Remembering Grandma.* Houston, TX: Pinata Books.

BERTRAND, DIANE G. 2003. *Family, Familia.* Houston, TX: Are Publico Press.

———. 2004. *My Pal, Victor.* Green Bay, WI: Raven Tree Press.

BRAMMER, ETHRIAM. 2003. *My Tata's Guitar.* Houston, TX: Pinata Books.

BUNTING, EVE. 1996. *Going Home.* New York: Harper/Trophy.

CAMERON, ANN. 1988. *The Most Beautiful Place in the World.* New York: Random House Children's Books.

DORROS, ARTHUR. 1991. *Abuela.* Dutton's Children's Books.

———. 1993. *Radio Man.* New York: HarperCollins.

HERRERA, JUAN FELIPE. 2004. *Featherless.* San Fransicso, CA: Children's Book Press.

MADRIGAL, ANTONIO HERNANDEZ. 1999. *Erandi's Braids.* New York: Putnam's.

MORA, PAT. 1990. *The Rainbow Tulip.* New York: Puffin Books.

———. 1992. *A Birthday Basket for Tia.* New York: Simon and Schuster.

PAULSEN, GARY. 1995. *The Tortilla Factory.* San Diego, CA: Harcourt Brace.

RYAN, PAM MUNOZ. 2000. *Esperanza's Rising.* New York: Scholastic.

SOTO, GARY. 1993. *Too Many Tamales.* New York: G. P. Putnam's Sons.

———. 1995. *Chato's Kitchen.* New York: Penguin Putnam.

URREA, LUIS ALBERTO. 2004. *The Devil's Highway: A True Story.* New York: Little Brown.

CONVENTIONS CHECKLIST

Name of Child	Conventions That Need Attention	Date

WEEKLY CHECKLIST

Name	Monday	Tuesday	Wednesday	Thursday	Friday
_____	_____	_____	_____	_____	_____
_____	_____	_____	_____	_____	_____
_____	_____	_____	_____	_____	_____
_____	_____	_____	_____	_____	_____
_____	_____	_____	_____	_____	_____
_____	_____	_____	_____	_____	_____
_____	_____	_____	_____	_____	_____
_____	_____	_____	_____	_____	_____
_____	_____	_____	_____	_____	_____
_____	_____	_____	_____	_____	_____
_____	_____	_____	_____	_____	_____
_____	_____	_____	_____	_____	_____

Key:

n   = new story

cs = continuous story

p   = publishing

l   = using random letters

es = using ending

ww = using whole words

s   = writing in sentences

Parts of Speech Checklist

Name	Noun	Verb	Adjective	Adverb	Preposition
___	___	___	___	___	___
___	___	___	___	___	___
___	___	___	___	___	___
___	___	___	___	___	___
___	___	___	___	___	___
___	___	___	___	___	___
___	___	___	___	___	___
___	___	___	___	___	___
___	___	___	___	___	___
___	___	___	___	___	___
___	___	___	___	___	___
___	___	___	___	___	___
___	___	___	___	___	___

Key:

D = Date

C = Comment

Looking for vivid use of these parts of speech.

Appendix K: Self-Assessment Checklists

HOW WELL AM I DOING AS A WRITER?

Date	I can do these things well.	These are the things I am working on.	These are the things I plan to learn.
_____	_____	_____	_____
_____	_____	_____	_____
_____	_____	_____	_____
_____	_____	_____	_____
_____	_____	_____	_____
_____	_____	_____	_____
_____	_____	_____	_____
_____	_____	_____	_____
_____	_____	_____	_____
_____	_____	_____	_____
_____	_____	_____	_____
_____	_____	_____	_____
_____	_____	_____	_____

CONVENTIONS AND CRAFTS I CAN DO LIKE A WRITER

Date I tried it . . .	What I tried to do . . .	What author did I get help from . . .

WRITING I DO

Date	Title and Type of Writing	Date Completed or Date I Put It Aside
——	————————	————————
——	————————	————————
——	————————	————————
——	————————	————————
——	————————	————————
——	————————	————————
——	————————	————————
——	————————	————————
——	————————	————————
——	————————	————————
——	————————	————————
——	————————	————————
——	————————	————————
——	————————	————————

Revision

Date	Type of Strategy I Tried	Title of Piece
_____	_____	_____
_____	_____	_____
_____	_____	_____
_____	_____	_____
_____	_____	_____
_____	_____	_____
_____	_____	_____
_____	_____	_____
_____	_____	_____
_____	_____	_____
_____	_____	_____
_____	_____	_____
_____	_____	_____
_____	_____	_____
_____	_____	_____

WRITING RUBRIC

Name _____ Date _____

Category	Consistent	Inconsistent	Comments
Able to write a coherent draft	_____	_____	_____
Willingly takes suggestions from peers and teacher	_____	_____	_____
Able to give constructive feedback to a peer's draft	_____	_____	_____
Attempts to incorporate colorful language	_____	_____	_____
Takes responsibility for revising	_____	_____	_____
Proofreads for _____	_____	_____	_____
Adheres to writing deadlines	_____	_____	_____
Keeps writing folder organized and up to date	_____	_____	_____
Uses conventions in meaningful ways	_____	_____	_____
Uses authors as mentors	_____	_____	_____
Uses writing time in constructive ways	_____	_____	_____

Final Grade _____

Grading system:

A–Consistent in all areas (9 out of 10)

B–Consistent in most areas (8 out of 10)

C–Consistent in many areas (7 out of 10)

D–Consistent in some areas (6 out of 10)

F–Inconsistent in many areas (3 or less out of 10)

FIRST STORY RUBRIC

Story Title _____

Please think about each item carefully. Then write in the box the number that best describes your writing. The teacher will also assess your story.

3 = I did an excellent job.
2 = I did an OK job.
1 = I did not do a very good job.
0 = I did not do this at all.

	Me	Teacher	Comments
There is evidence of prewriting. I used a web, drawing, list, conversation, etc. to organize my thoughts.			
There is evidence of revision. I met with at least one other person to get their praise, questions, and suggestions.			
There is evidence of editing. I met with at least one person to correct punctuation, capitalization, etc. I am showing respect for my audience.			
I have a beginning sentence that grabs the reader's attention.			
My story has a clear beginning, middle, and end.			
My story has complete sentences. I do not have any run-on sentences.			
I do not have lots of *ands* in my story.			
I have an ending sentence to close the door on my story.			
TOTALS			

Children's Literature Bibliography

BUNTING, EVE. 1991. *Fly Away Home.* New York: Clarion Books.

———. 1994. *A Day's Work.* New York: Clarion Books.

———. 1994. *Smoky Nights.* New York: Harcourt.

COWLEY, JOY. 1990. *A Monster Sandwich.* Bothell, WA: Wright Group.

———. 1997. *Singing Down the Rain.* New York: HarperCollins.

CREWS, NINA. 2004. *The Neighborhood Mother Goose.* New York: Greenwillow.

DORROS, ARTHUR. 1991. *Abuela.* New York: Dutton's Children's Books.

EDGERTON, CLYDE. 1987. *Walking Across Egypt.* Chapel Hill, NC: Algonquin Books.

ESTES, ELINOR. 1944. *100 Dresses.* New York: Harcourt.

FOX, MEM. 1989. *Feathers and Fool.* New York: Harcourt.

———. 2004. *Green Sheep.* Orlando, FL: Harcourt.

GIFF, PATRICIA. 1984. *Kids of the Polk Street School.* New York: Random House.

GRAY, LIBBA MOORE. 1995. *My Mama Had a Dancing Heart.* New York: Orchard Books.

GRIEGO, MARGOT C. 1988. *Tortillitas Para Mama.* New York: Holt.

LAMINACK, LESTER. 2004. *Saturdays and Teacakes.* Atlanta, GA: Peachtree.

MCKISSACK, PATRICIA. 2001. *Goin' Someplace Special.* New York: Atheneum.

MACLACHLEN, PATRICIA. 1994. *All the Places to Love.* New York: Harper.

MERRIAM, EVE. 1999. *The Wise Woman and Her Secret.* New York: Simon and Schuster.

NUMEROFF, LAURA. 1985. *If You Give a Mouse a Cookie.* New York: Harper and Row.

POLACCO, PATRICIA. 1990. *Thunder Cake.* New York: Philomel Books.

——. 1992. *Chicken Sunday.* New York: Philomel Books.

——. 1994. *My Rotten Red-Headed Older Brother.* New York: Philomel Books.

——. 1998. *Thank You, Mr. Falker.* New York: Philomel Books.

RYLANT, CYNTHIA. 1992. *Missing May.* New York: Bantam Doubleday.

SHANNON, DAVID. 1998. *No, David.* New York: Blue Sky Press.

UCHIDA, YOSHIKO. 1981. *A Jar of Dreams.* New York: Simon and Schuster.

WOODSON, JACQUELINE. 1998. *We Had a Picnic Last Sunday Past.* New York: Hyperion.

——. 2001. *The Other Side.* New York: Putnam's Books.

YOLEN, JANE. 1997. *Miz Berlin Walks.* New York: Philomel Books.

YOUNG, ED. 1968. *Chinese Mother Goose.* Cleveland, OH: World Publishing Co.

Bibliography

ATWELL, NANCIE. 1998. *In the Middle.* Portsmouth, NH: Heinemann.

———. 2004. Writer's Notebooks: Managing Students' Development of Important Tools for Thinking. Presented at Mid-South Reading and Writing Institute, 18–19 June, Birmingham, AL.

BOMER, RANDY, AND KATHERINE BOMER. 2001. *For a Better World: Reading and Writing for Social Action.* Portsmouth, NH: Heinemann.

BONILLA, C.A., J. GOSS, AND K. L. LAUDERDALE, EDS. 1999. *Students at Risk: Poverty, Pregnancy, Violence, Depression, and the Demise of the Traditional Family.* Stockton, CA: ICA Inc.

BROWN, DAVE F. 2001. *Becoming a Successful Urban Teacher.* Portsmouth, NH: Heinemann.

BROWN, THOMAS J. 1999. *Teaching the Poor and Children of Color.* Columbia, MD: Brown and Associates.

BULLOUGH, ROBERT V. 2001. *Uncertain Lives: Children of Promise, Teachers of Hope.* New York: Teachers College Press.

CALKINS, LUCY M. 1994. *The Art of Teaching Writing.* Portsmouth, NH: Heinemann.

CAMBOURNE, BRIAN. 2002. *"The Conditions of Learning: Is Learning Natural?" Reading Teacher* 55 (8): 758–62.

COMPTON-LILLY, CATHERINE. 2004. *Confronting Racism, Poverty, and Power: Classroom Strategies to Change the World.* Portsmouth, NH: Heinemann.

DELPIT, LISA. 1995. *Other People's Children: Cultural Conflict in the Classroom.* New York: The New Press.

FEDERAL INTERAGENCY FORUM ON CHILD AND FAMILY STATISTICS. 2002. *America's Children: Key National Indicators of Well-Being.* Washington, D.C.: U.S. Government Printing Office.

FLETCHER, RALPH. 1996. *Breathing In Breathing Out.* Portsmouth, NH: Heinemann.

GOOD, THOMAS, AND JERRE BROPHY. 1994. *Looking in Classrooms,* 6th ed. New York: HarperCollins College Publishers.

GRAVES, DONALD H. 1983. *Writing: Teachers and Children at Work.* Portsmouth, NH: Heinemann.

——. 1994. *A Fresh Look at Writing.* Portsmouth, NH: Heinemann.

HODGKINSON, HAROLD L. 1995. *"What Should We Call People? Race, Class, and the Census for 2000."* Kappan 77 (2): 173-79.

JONES, STEPHANIE. 2004. "Living Poverty and Literacy Learning: Sanctioning Topics of Students' Lives." *Language Arts* 81 (6): 461-69.

KIRKLAND, LYNN. 2004. Do You Encourage or Discourage the Development of Language in Your Classroom? Presented at Mid-South Reading and Writing Institute, 18-19 June, Birmingham, AL.

KNAPP, MICHAEL E., AND PATRICK M. SHIELDS. 1990. "Reconceiving Academic Instructions for the Children of Poverty." *Phi Delta Kappan* 71 (10): 753-58.

MANIATES, HELEN, BETTY DOERR, AND MARGARET GOLDEN. 2001. *Teach Our Children Well: Essential Strategies for the Urban Classroom.* Portsmouth, NH: Heinemann.

MOFFETT, JAMES. 1968. *Teaching the Universe of Discourse.* Boston: Houghton Mifflin.

MOORE, K. A., S. VANDIVERE, AND J. EHRLE. 2000. *Socioeconomic Risk and Child Well-Being.* Washington, D.C.: Urban Institute, Child Trends Inc.

MURRAY, DONALD M. 1978. *Internal Revision: A Process of Discovery.* In C. R. Cooper and L. Odell (eds). *Research on Composing* (pp. 184-207). Urbana, IL: NCTE.

NATIONAL READING PANEL. 2000. *Teaching Children to Read.* Washington, D.C.: National Institute of Child Health and Human Development Clearinghouse.

NITKO, ANTHONY J. 2004. *Educational Assessment of Students,* 4th ed. Columbus, OH: Pearson.

PETERSON, M. E. 1997. Low-SES Literacy Backgrounds: Effects on Formal Schooling. ERIC ED 408 559.

POPHAM, W. JAMES. 2001. *The Truth About Testing.* Alexandria, VA: Association for Supervision and Curriculum Development.

——. 2002. *Classroom Assessment: What Teachers Need to Know,* 3rd ed. Boston, MA: Allyn and Bacon.

PURCELL-GATES, V., AND K. L. DAHL. 1989. Patterns of Success and Failure in Literacy Learning Among Low-SES Urban Children in Traditional Skills-Based Kindergarten and First Grade Classrooms. Paper presented at National Reading Conference. ERIC ED 325 800.

RAY, KATIE WOOD. 2001. *The Writing Workshop: Working Through the Hard Parts.* Urbana, IL: National Council of Teachers of English.

———. 2002. *What You Know by Heart: How to Develop Curriculum for Your Writing Workshop.* Portsmouth, NH: Heinemann.

REED, SALLY, AND R. CRAIG SAULTER. 1990. "Children of Poverty: The Status of 12 Million Young Americans." *Phi Delta Kappan* 71 (10): K1-K12.

SHANNON, PATRICK. 1998. *Reading Poverty.* Portsmouth, NH: Heinemann.

SHERMAN, ARLOC. 1997. *Poverty Matters: The Cost of Child Poverty in America.* Children's Defense Fund. Washington, D.C.

SCHEURICH, J. J. 1998. "Highly Successful and Loving Public Elementary Schools Populated Mainly by Low-SES Children of Color." *Urban Education* 33 (4): 451-91.

SOLLEY, BOBBIE A. 2000. *Writing Workshop: Reflection of Elementary and Middle School Teachers.* Boston, MA: Allyn and Bacon.

TAYLOR, DENNY. 1998. *Family Literacy: Young Children Learning to Read and Write.* Portsmouth, NH: Heinemann.

WORTHY, JO, AND KAREN BROADDUS. 2002. "Fluency Beyond the Primary Grades: From Group Performance to Silent, Independent Reading." *The Reading Teacher* 55: 334-43.